BUDDHISTS TALK ABOUT JESUS
CHRISTIANS TALK ABOUT THE BUDDHA

BUDDHISTS TALK ABOUT JESUS

CHRISTIANS TALK ABOUT THE BUDDHA

Edited by

Rita M. Gross
and Terry C. Muck

Continuum
New York   London

2000

The Continuum International Publishing Group Inc
370 Lexington Avenue, New York, NY 10017

The Continuum International Publishing Group Ltd
Wellington House, 125 Strand, London WC2R OBB

Originally published as *Buddhist-Christian Studies* 19 (1999)
© by University of Hawai'i Press
Introduction © 1999 by Rita M. Gross
"Buddhist Books on Jesus" © 1999 by Terry C. Muck

Printed in the United States of America

Library of Congress Cataloging-in-Publication Data

Buddhists talk about Jesus, Christians talk about the Buddha / edited by Rita M. Gross and
Terry C. Muck.
    p.   cm.
   ISBN 0-8264-1196-7
   1. Jesus—Buddhist interpretations.. 2. Christianity and other religions—Buddhism.
3. Buddhism—Relations—Christianity.   I. Gross, Rita M.   II. Muck, Terry C., 1947–
BT304.914.B83   2000
261.2 43—dc21   99-056981

Contents

Introduction

Rita M. Gross

University of Wisconsin—Eau Claire

THIS BOOK IS the result of multiple collaborations. The first collaboration is that which occurs between the co-editors of the *Buddhist-Christian Studies Journal,* in which these essays first appeared. One of us is a Buddhist, the other a Christian; both of us have significant familiarity with the other tradition. One of us is a man, the other a woman. These balances are indicative of careful policies of religious and gender balance characteristic of the Society for Buddhist-Christian Studies, the organization whose journal we co-edit. We have found our collaboration to be rewarding, enriching, and mutually fulfilling, both professionally and personally. Clearly, our experience indicates that people of different, but equally intense, religious persuasions and temperaments can work together to promote harmony and understanding.

When Terry Muck and myself began to collaborate on co-editing the *Journal,* we immediately decided that we wanted to try some experiments in the *Journal,* including thematically focused issues for which we would solicit contributions. We wanted to encourage honest expression of opinions and conclusions, including especially what we find troubling about the tradition with which we are in dialogue. We are convinced that, just as meaningful inter-religious dialogue cannot be a covert missionary enterprise, in which each partner in the pseudo-dialogue tries to convince the other of the superiority of her or his own religion, so also meaningful inter-religious dialogue must be more than a polite mutual-admiration society. Though usually we dialoguers are quite familiar with the other tradition, most of us in inter-religious dialogue identify with one of the traditions in dialogue. Therefore, there must be something about that other tradition that troubles us or that we do not find personally convincing. We believe that Buddhist-Christian dialogue has reached a level of trust and respect that warrants discussing these troubling dimensions of the other tradition openly. We also expect that having Christians discuss an aspect of Buddhism and Buddhists discuss an aspect of Christianity would result in insights into both traditions that would not be likely if each dialogue partner discusses only his or her own religion—the more usual format for inter-religious dialogue. For our first such experiment, we decided to ask contributors to discuss candidly and openly, both positively and negatively, but without a triumphalist agenda, the most well-known figure of each tradition—Jesus and the Buddha. We asked four Buddhist scholar-practitioners to write about Jesus and four Christian scholar-practitioners to write about the Buddha. These experimental-experiential discussions are then commented upon by two Christians discussing Buddhist perceptions of Jesus and two Buddhists discussing Christian perceptions of the Buddha. We have also included co-editor Terry Muck's discussion of three recent books written about Jesus by prominent Buddhists including the Dalai Lama and Thich Nhat Hanh. Thus, this dialogue represents a dense interplay of several levels of commentary and reflection. The quality of the collaboration between the various authors and commentators, and between the editors of the volume and the contributors to it, demonstrates well the emotional and doctrinal maturity of Buddhist-Christian dialogue. We thank each of our contributors profusely for their interesting, original insights into these two major religious traditions.

Yet another level of collaboration occurred between the University of Hawai'i Press, which publishes the *Buddhist-Christian Studies Journal,* in which these essays originally appeared, and Continuum Press, which published them in book format to make them more widely accessible. We are grateful to both presses for their willingness to work with each other to make this experiment in dialogue, which is only the first of its type, more widely available.

Though this experiment is limited by its small number of participants, some reasonably consistent and interesting common themes can be seen in the essays that follow. First, without exception, the Buddhists had difficulties with Christian claims about Jesus, though all expressed admiration for the human being that they saw in the records about him, particularly the gospels. The most often expressed difficulty stems from the frequent Christian claims concerning Jesus' uniqueness or his universal relevance to all humans. José Cabezón suggests that Buddhists do not have problems with the claim that Jesus is a manifestation of a deity, but with the claim that he is the only such manifestation. Rita Gross devotes much of her chapter to critiquing Christian claims about Jesus' unique and exclusive relevance for all humans and providing an alternative to such exclusive truth claims. Bokin Kim repeatedly suggests that she can respect Jesus as *a* way, but not as *the* way. And she repeatedly suggests that Christ and the Buddha are religious equivalents in the religious lives of Christians and Buddhists. Among the Buddhists, only Soho Machida focuses much more on other issues, though he also states that "there is no one truth and there is no one superior religion. This simple fact must be humbly accepted by Christians who think otherwise."

Because of the Buddhists' emphasis on Christian claims about Jesus' uniqueness and exclusive relevance to humanity, the two Christian respondents also focus on this issue. Both eschew traditional Christian exclusive truth claims and Marcus Borg suggests, based on his experiences of meeting many Christians through his lectures, that many mainline Christians are giving up traditional exclusive truth claims. Both Marcus Borg and Dominic Crossan suggest that the language of Jesus as *the* savior or *the* decisive manifestation of the divine means that Jesus is indeed decisive, *for Christians alone.* Dominic Crossan posits that there is an inevitable human slippage from *a* to *the*. This, he suggests, is only a problem if "it is taken literally and the other equally relative absolutes of others are negated."

Interestingly, for the Christians who wrote essays regarding their impressions of the Buddha, the issue of Jesus' unique and universal relevance for all humans does not arise. Their reasons for ultimately preferring Jesus to the Buddha, despite their genuine admiration of and respect for the Buddha, stem not from an abstract claim that Jesus is necessary for *everyone*, but from the personal experience that Jesus is necessary for *them*, that Buddhist claims about the impossibility of external salvation or vicarious atonement simply do not work for them spiritually.

If anything, the Christians' admiration of the Buddha exceed the Buddhists' admiration for Jesus as human being. All the Christian commentators express profound personal experiences with the Buddha and report that some encounter with the Buddha and Buddhism not only changed them personally but deepened their understanding of and appreciation for Christianity. Yet, except for Donald Swearer, all the Christians explicitly state that at some point, Jesus as Savior is necessary in their spiritual lives. Bonnie Thurston is most forceful in her declaration: "The Buddha directs me away from himself. The Christ invites me to himself. In the Four Reliances the Buddha teaches, 'rely on the teaching not the teacher.' In Christianity the teaching *is* the teacher." A few sentences later, regarding the famous Buddhist command "Be ye lamps unto yourselves," she writes, "I know from bitter experience my own inability to be my own lamp." The Christians adopt the Buddhist language of "self power" and "other power" and declare that self power does not work and is not sufficient in their own experience; instead other power is necessary and Jesus, as incarnation of god and savior of humanity, provides that other power.

Just as the Christian respondents commented primarily on the Buddhists' main issue with Jesus and claims about him, so also the Buddhist respondents to the Christians comment on the main point made by Christians. Both Grace Burford and Taitetsu Unno discuss the Christians' declaration of their need for "other power," but their insights are quite different. Grace Burford does not reject help and the grace of interdependence as part of the spiritual journey, but she declares, ". . . give me a map, lend me your car (or raft?), show me a shortcut, even protect me along the way if you can, but do not make the trip for me!" By this she means that experiencing a need for vicarious atonement or a need to have an innate deficiency fixed by someone else are not religious outlooks that she can adopt for herself. Taitetsu Unno, on the other hand, suggests that the Buddha is not only "human through and through," but also a "numinous" presence. The enlightenment experience goes well beyond the ordinary human experiences of rationality and discursiveness and cannot be comprehended by these faculties. As an enlightened being, the Buddha, or any other enlightened being, is an embodiment of the *dharma*, the truth. Taitetsu Unno suggests that the Buddhist recommendation "Be ye lamps unto yourselves," which Bonnie Thurston and other Christians claim they simply cannot do, must be understood properly. "The self here is not the unenlightened ego-self, but the enlightened non-ego self imbued with *dhamma.*" Relying on our unlighted ego-selves will get us nowhere. The self that is to be our lamp is the enlightened numinous non-ego self which transcends rationality, discursiveness, and ego-based striving.

Interestingly, claims for Jesus' divinity are not troubling to some of the Buddhists, especially those of Mahayana orientation. José Cabezón appreciates Jesus as a magician who has unusual powers; such figures are not unknown in Asian religions, including Buddhism. He also explains Mahayana Buddhist beliefs that " the universe is populated by a wide range of deities" and goes on to suggest that ". . . at least Mahayana Buddhists find little that is objectionable in the notion that Jesus is the manifestation of a deity, or the embodiment of a particular quality or attribute. . . ." Taitetsu Unno's declaration that an enlightened Buddha is more than "human through and through," if by "human" we mean the ordinary ego-self, has already been mentioned.

The problems Buddhists would have with Christian claims about deity are stated succinctly by José Cabezón. "What Buddhists find objectionable is (a) the Christian characterization of the deity whose manifestation Jesus is said to be, and (b) the claim that Jesus is unique in being such a manifestation." With these two objections, we return, at least tangentially, to issues already discussed—Christian claims about Jesus' unique and universal relevance, and the Christian experience of the need for "other power." The issue of Jesus' unique and universal significance has already been discussed quite extensively, but José Cabezón's summary of what Buddhists might find objectionable about the deity of whom Jesus is said to be an embodiment is instructive. "There is no god who is the creator of the universe, who is originally pure and primordially perfected, who is omnipotent and who can will the salvation of beings. Jesus, therefore, cannot be the incarnation of such a God." Of this list of objections from a Buddhist point of view, the claim that the Christian authors focus upon concerns the existence of a deity who could "will the salvation of beings," though Christians would be unlikely to use that phrasing in describing the salvation and liberation they find in and through Jesus.

Several striking contrasts between the Buddhist and the Christian authors are apparent in these essays. First, the Christians' testimonial concerning how much they have learned from Buddhism for their Christian spiritual lives is far greater than any reverse testimonial. In fact, though all the Buddhists express appreciation for Jesus, none of them mentions personal spiritual growth that is the result of an encounter with Jesus or with Christianity. This asymmetry may result from the difference between typical Christian and Buddhist practices regarding missionary activity and proselytization. Because Buddhists usually don't proselytize, Christians may feel safer in their experiments with Buddhism; it is unlikely that they will experience pressure from Buddhists to become Buddhist if they like and admire the Buddha. But Buddhists may not feel the same safety and freedom regarding experiments with Christianity and a relationship with Jesus. And, because of their own history, responsible Christians may emphasize their appreciation for non-Christian religions, Buddhism in this case. But this asymmetry could also stem from the fact that because Buddhists don't claim that the Buddha is a deity who creates and saves humanity, Christians can take on aspects of Buddhism and admire the Buddha as human teacher without in any way compromising their loyalty to the deity of Christianity incarnate in Jesus. The reverse is not true for Buddhists. Christians do claim that Jesus is the incarnation of a deity who creates and redeems the world and such claims run counter to essential Buddhist ideas about how the world works.

We invited authors to be quite direct in their evaluations of the other tradition, and we expected authors to make comments about the other tradition, even to suggest revisions in the other tradition, that would probably not be made by an insider. A second contrast between Buddhist and Christian essayists is that the Buddhists were much bolder in their comments about Jesus and their assessments of Christianity than were the Christians in their comments about the Buddha and Buddhism. Soho Machida's intriguing title "Jesus, Man of Sin" amply demonstrates Buddhist willingness to suggest revisions to basics of Christian theology. Soho Machida suggests that Jesus' cry of despair, "My God, my God, why have you deserted me?" not be glossed over or explained away and he suggests that for Jesus to share humanity with us, he must share the original sin that is the lot of every human being, according to classical Christian theology. And revision to another classic tenet of Christian theology is suggested by Soho Machida. ". . . why did Jesus have to experience the suffering of crucifixion? . . . Jesus was crucified to atone for his own sin. He courageously showed us the way each of us must take responsibility for our own lives."

Rita Gross also takes a rather critical approach to Christian claims about Jesus, especially claims about his unique and universal relevance, as has already been noted. She too suggests how Christian theology might correct itself on this point. José Cabezón argues that, though Jesus could be an incarnation of a deity, he could not be an incarnation of the kind of deity that Christians posit and encourages Christians to rethink with what deity Jesus should be associated. José Cabezón also recounts a conversation between one of his Buddhist teachers and a Christian colleague. His Buddhist teacher had asked the Christian to explain something of Christianity to him and burst out in laughter at what he heard. The Buddhist teacher's basic question: "How can the death of one individual act as the direct and substantive cause for the salvation of others?"

The Christians were much gentler with the Buddha and Buddhism. Terry Muck comes the closest to finding a problem with the Buddha. It bothers him that the Buddha abandoned his wife and young son in his quest for liberation and enlightenment, but Terry Muck also respects the Buddha more for this "weakness." In this weakness, the Buddha is like many Biblical heroes who did not completely solve "the puzzle of interlocking commitment to ideals and relational truth." For the most part, however, rather than being bothered by claims about the Buddha or suggesting revisions to Buddhist theology, the Christians focused on their appreciation for Buddha and Buddhism. Again, perhaps this contrast stems from Christianity's history of proselytization. Perhaps the Christian essayists felt that now is the time for Christians to listen to and learn from other religions, rather than to criticize and correct them.

We should also note, even emphasize, that Buddhists and Christians share an important evaluation of the other tradition in common. Without exception, Buddhist authors express respect for Jesus' selfless work on behalf of others and his social teachings. Christians evaluate the Buddha in the same way, noting his refusal to adhere to the Indian caste system, his wisdom in organizing his religious institution, the Buddhist sangha, and even his relative openness to women, considering the culture and times in which he worked. In these troubled times of great suffering and danger, this common concern with human well-being may be more important than any other claims, issues, or considerations.

JESUS CHRIST THROUGH BUDDHIST EYES

A God, but Not a Savior

JOSÉ IGNACIO CABEZÓN
Iliff School of Theology

T HE ADAGE ABOUT "location, location, location" as an operative principle is perhaps as true in theology as it is in other more mundane ventures. For a theologian, identifying one's location principally involves situating oneself with respect to one's religious tradition, but also vis-à-vis the secular currents of the past and present that have been for one intellectually influential. I take my task in this essay to be a theological one, and so perhaps it is not wholly out of place to begin with a few words concerning my theological location. Of the various hats I wear, one of the most important is the one that identifies me as an academic Buddhist theologian, one who works from out of the Indo-Tibetan tradition.[1] As a Buddhist, my theological location has been largely shaped by the years that I spent as a monk in the Byes College of the exiled Tibetan Buddhist monastic University of Sera in southern India, where I received the bulk of my training in the classical textual tradition of Indo-Tibetan Mahayana Buddhism. As an academic, I have been molded by the Western buddhological tradition, with its strong emphasis on the philological study of texts, albeit tempered by the other concerns (e.g., material culture, social life, and a variety of theoretical issues) that are at the core of contemporary North American approaches to Buddhist studies.[2]

My theological identity is determined not only by my chosen tradition and academic discipline, however, but also by my commitment to interreligious dialogue. Dialogue, especially with the Christian tradition, informs and shapes my theology at the level of content. In this regard I have benefited greatly from the fact that I teach at a Christian seminary and that I am fortunate enough to have colleagues who are similarly committed to the intellectual value of the cross-cultural and interreligious exchange of ideas. In addition to influencing the intellectual content of my theology, dialogue also informs my religious life. The only religious praxis community with which I am presently affiliated is a community of Buddhists and Christians who meet on a weekly basis for a contemplative service that includes a common liturgy, readings from the two traditions, and periods of silent meditation.[3]

No less important a part of my theological location is the fact that I was raised a Cuban Catholic. I rejected Christianity at an early age largely on philosophical grounds, and this no doubt opened up the space for my eventually embracing Buddhism. Nonetheless, I continue to this day to cherish many aspects of Latino-Catholic culture—its malleability and especially its ability to accommodate magic, its mystical bent, the passion of its piety, its emphasis on tradition and ritual, the richness of its art—and this too, without a doubt, has influenced my theological worldview.

In what follows, readers will undoubtedly see in my mode of engaging the question my commitment to the historical-critical method, which is the result of my training as a buddhologist. They will see in the content of my response the doctrinal voice of Indo-Tibetan Mahayana Buddhism, my tradition of choice. In the organization of the essay and in its (alas, unfulfilled) wish to be complete, they will witness my penchant for scholastic systematicity, the legacy of my Tibetan Buddhist monastic training. They will also encounter a Jesus, or perhaps Jesuses, that are the result of (others') historical and textual study of the Christian sources. But within each of these Jesuses there is bound to be evident at least a glimmer of the Cuban Christ of my youth, the one Jesus that, over and above all of the others, I know most intimately.

If the identification of my location as a theological respondent is important, so too is the location of the object to which I am responding. More so now than at any other point of history, the location of Jesus is something that cannot be taken for granted. As Sheila Davaney says in her characterization of the work of Dominic Crossan:[4] "Not only is historical material difficult to come by in relation to Jesus but, Crossan insists, what material we have represents value-laden interpretations yielding different and even contradictory portrayals of Jesus. From the beginning, according to Crossan, the various Christs of faith emerged, and the historical Jesus is available to us only within and through those theological portrayals."[5]

My response in this essay is mediated theologically by my subjectivity as respondent, but it is equally mediated theologically by the portrayal of Jesus, who is the object of my response. In what follows I take myself to have chosen a relatively mainstream Jesus as the object of my reflections, realizing all the while that, especially in this hyperhistoricist, critical, and skeptical age, such a portrayal may be outmoded. How plausible my portrayal of Jesus is will have to be determined by those for whom Jesus stands as an object of faith and devotion. (I take the plausibility of the Jesus that we Buddhists have chosen as the object of our response to be at least part of the Christian respondents' task in this volume.) In any case, it is my hope that the Jesus I have chosen to represent will not be wholly a figment of my imagination, and that instead my portrayal (even if not my assessment) of Jesus will be one that is familiar to a relatively large number of Christians.

JESUS AS SOCIAL ACTIVIST AND CRITIC

THIS ASPECT OF Jesus' identity has of course been emphasized by many New Testament scholars and has been the basis for entire movements such as liberation theology. It is said to be exemplified in Jesus' espousal of a radical egalitarianism, "something infinitely more terrifying than (contemporary democracy),"[6] in his repudiation of class boundaries, in his antihierarchical views, in his skepticism about institutions, and in his empathy with and prioritizing of the cause of the poor and downtrodden of society.

Like Christianity, Buddhism also began as a reformist movement, but of a very different kind. Unlike Jesus, the Buddha was not a peasant; his followers seem to have been principally middle- and upper-middle-class men and women, as was his principal audience; and his criticisms were primarily directed at the Brahminical religious beliefs and practices prevalent in his day, not at the social structures that marginalized and oppressed men and women in ancient India.[7] This is not to say that the Buddha was unconcerned with social issues, or that his teachings do not have social implications, or that they have not been used in history to socially reconstructive ends,[8] but it is clear his goal was, rather than to transform the existing social order, to use it to further his religious ends. For example, whereas mendicancy—that is, religious itineracy—in other societies represented a flight from the social order and even a vehicle for social protest, it is clear that in India, at least by the time of the Buddha, it had already achieved a socially legitimized and institutionalized form.

This being said, there are clear parallels between the Buddha and Jesus as regards their reformist tendencies, and this certainly gives Buddhists a vehicle and framework for appreciating Jesus. The Buddha opened up the religious life (and therefore the possibility of salvation) to members of society that had hitherto been denied it: members of the lowest castes and women especially. Both figures were also exponents of a kind of theological reform that emphasized the interior life over external action. Nonetheless, as a program of social reform, Jesus' must be recognized as being the more radical and far-reaching, and this no doubt is why the Christian tradition to this day, even when impeded by its own institutional forms, has been at the forefront of social transformation.

Speaking personally now, I must say that this is for me one of the most appealing aspects of the legacy of Jesus. I consider my Christian brothers and sisters fortunate, and I rejoice in the fact that they have at the very core of their tradition—in the very life of their founder—such a clear and superb model for what it means to be a socially responsible person, a person of integrity, in the world. We Buddhists have a great deal to learn from this aspect of the life of Jesus.

Jesus as Magician

I INCLUDE WITHIN this aspect of the life of Jesus his various miracles, his exorcisms, his work as a healer, and even his resurrection. As regards these events, there are for the Buddhist tradition, as there have been in the West, two possible types of response. The first challenges the historicity or veracity of these events. It would attribute them to superstition or to later tradition, and, in its desire to make of Jesus either a charlatan or a paradigm of enlightened rationalism, it strips him of this aspect of his identity. I opt here for the second alternative: to take these events as historically factual. While doing so, however, I beg to differ with those Christians who consider these events as probative of various aspects of Christian theological dogma. That Jesus had these powers—that he could cure the sick, manipulate matter, cast out demons, raise others (and himself be raised) from the dead—most certainly points to the fact that he was an extraordinary individual. None of these events are for Buddhists outside of the realm of possibility. At the same time, they are not unique in history, nor is the person possessing these attributes unique. More important, they do not prove that such a person is God or that he or she is enlightened or worthy of worship.

Magic as such is theologically neutral for Buddhists. Most, and perhaps all, of the extraordinary feats performed by Jesus would be classified by Buddhists as "common accomplishments" (*thun mongs ba'i dngos grub*): common because they are feats that can be accomplished by Buddhists and non-Buddhists alike, requiring a certain degree of meditative competence, but no real degree of permanent spiritual maturity. This being said, the fact that Jesus performed these various actions for the benefit of others *does* point to an important fact; namely, that he was operating from an altruistic motivation, and this perhaps is the more important point for Buddhists: not that Jesus was a *magician,* but that he was a *loving* one.

I have always found it awkward to offer theological advice to a tradition that is not my own, even if, as I have mentioned above, it is a religious tradition that is an important part of my past and that I still hold dear to my heart. Given that the editors of this book have encouraged us to do so, however, I offer this guarded counsel, modulated autobiographically. My attraction to Tibetan Buddhism in large part is due to the fact that it is an unabashedly magical religion. In this sterile space of skepticism that is (post)modernity, I find it refreshing that my tradition is a place of mystery, a magical refuge inhabited by all sorts of spirits, a space where extraordinary events abound. This has certainly enlivened my religious life. Might magic do the same for Christians? Certainly there is precedent for this in the Christian tradition, in the life of Jesus but also in the life of the saints, and even in some aspects of liturgy. To attribute Jesus' magic to his divinity, it seems to me, has relegated magic to the transcendental sphere, making it inaccessible to those who need it most: us. Perhaps it is time to allow magic to enter Christian life in greater abundance.

JESUS AS TEACHER

I WOULD VENTURE to guess that of all of the aspects of the persona of Jesus that I deal with in this essay, none is more appealing to Buddhists than that of Jesus *magister*. This may say more about Buddhists than it does about Jesus, however, for Buddhists, at least scholastic Buddhists, have always seen the teachings of their master(s) as embodied in the concept they call *dharma* as constituting the core of their tradition. Hence, of the three refuges—Buddha, dharma, and *sangha*—it is the dharma that is considered the true (*dngos*) refuge. The doctor (Buddha) may diagnose the problem and prescribe the cure, the nursing staff (*sangha*) may administer it and help the patient in the process of recovery, but it is the medicine (dharma, as embodied in the Buddha's teachings and internalized in the lives of his followers) that is the real antidote to the illness.

Of course, a thorough Buddhist response to Jesus as teacher requires nothing less than a full assessment of his teachings. This is not possible here due to constraints of space. Such an assessment is further complexified by the fact that what constitutes the authentic teachings of Jesus are highly contested, having become for New Testament scholars a source of almost obsessive preoccupation. This being said, there are certain portions of Jesus' teachings—portions on which there seems to be at least partial consensus concerning authenticity[9]— that I believe resonate well with Buddhist doctrine. These include at least portions of the so-called beatitudes (Mark 5:3–10).[10] Equally attractive are the apparently authentic teachings of Jesus concerning love of the enemy (Matt. 5:43–48; Luke 6:27–28, 32–35), his admonition to repay evil with kindness, and his advocacy of charity (Matt. 5:38–42; Luke 6:29–30, 18:22) and of equanimity (Luke 10:30–35), all of which resonate well with the Mahayana Buddhist teachings on the virtues of universal and impartial compassion and with the perfections (*paramita*) of patience and giving. Mention should also be made of Jesus' emphasis on self- rather than other-directed criticism (Matt.

7:1–5; Luke 6:36–42; Thomas 26), as well as his counsel to followers concerning the importance of renouncing a life dedicated to the pursuit of wealth in favor of a simple itinerant's life dedicated to the pursuit of virtue through humility (Mark 6:8–10, 8:34–36, 9:35, 10:23–25, 29–31, 10:42–45; Matt. 6:25–34, 19:23–24; Luke 9:23–27, 10:1–9, 12:16–31; Thomas 14, 36, 63), all of which resonate well with the Buddhist monastic ideal.

While there is much that is appealing in what Jesus taught, there also appear to be lacunae in what Buddhists would expect to find in the collected teachings of a sage. For example, there is evinced in the extant material little concern for the welfare of living beings other than human beings. There is a lack of detailed teaching setting forth a systematic path to salvation, and, perhaps most disturbing, there is little or no mention of wisdom or gnosis, which for Buddhists is the very heart of the spiritual path.[11] Of course, it might be the case that many of Jesus' teachings have been lost, and Gnostic teachings are indeed found among the New Testament apocryphal texts. Still, it is surprising to Buddhists that especially the idea of wisdom or gnosis should have been so marginalized by Christians.[12]

In addition to what, from a Buddhist perspective, appear to be lacunae in the canonical teachings of Jesus, there is some material that *is* found in the canonical sources that seems quite foreign to Buddhists. Perhaps the best example is all of the apparently authentic material concerning the kingdom or imperial rule of God. Buddhists will obviously find this material problematic in part because of the deity whose kingdom is being prophesied (see below). Aside from this, however, I believe it fair to say that Buddhists also find the particular brand of Christian apocalypticism to be problematic. This is not to say that quasi-apocalyptic doctrines are unknown to Buddhists.[13] What Buddhists find disturbing is the utter finality of the Christian apocalypse, which represents a break in history after which the fate of human beings is forever sealed. Such a notion is anathema to Buddhists principally because it implies that there exists a time after which the potential for the salvation of at least some beings becomes nullified. From a Buddhist perspective, history as we know it simply cannot come to an end until all beings have been liberated.[14]

Of course, a great deal more could be said about which portions of the teachings of Jesus do and do not resonate with Buddhist doctrine. But perhaps this impressionistic treatment of the subject is sufficient to allow the reader at least a glimpse of the complexity of some of the issues.

JESUS AS GOD

ARGUABLY THE SINGLE most problematic aspect of Jesus' identity for Buddhists is his portrayal by Christians as God. I believe, however, that the nature of the Buddhist reluctance in this regard has often been misunderstood. The problem lies not in the claim that Jesus is the incarnation or manifestation of a deity. What Buddhists find objectionable is (a) the Christian characterization of the deity whose manifestation Jesus is said to be and (b) the claim that Jesus is unique in being such a manifestation.

Mahayana Buddhists believe that the universe is populated by a wide range of deities. Some of these are not more than spirits, who, like humans and animals, are subject to the vicissitudes of karma, and hence still bound in the cycle of rebirth (*samsara*).[15] Nonetheless, because of previous spiritual accomplishments, many of these deities have developed the ability to manifest a variety of physical forms.[16] Other deities, those who have attained the state of perfection known as enlightenment (*bodhi*), have gone beyond the cycle of involuntary rebirth. Such "supramundane" deities—beings who have attained the state of buddhahood—also have the ability to manifest such forms, but in a much more highly developed fashion. The historical buddhas who manifest on the earth for the betterment of humankind are in fact considered the incarnations or manifestations (*nirmana-* or *nairmanika-kayas*) of subtle, nonphysical "bodies" (*dharmakayas*).[17] Moreover, especially in the Buddhist Tantric tradition, there is the notion that enlightened beings can create special incarnations that are embodiments of selective aspects of the enlightened state. Hence, Manjusri is considered to be the physical manifestation of enlightened wisdom (*prajna*),[18] Tara to be the physical manifestation of enlightened power (*samarthya*), and so forth. In Tibet it is also not uncommon to find situations in which three different historical figures were (and are) identified as the body, speech, and mind incarnations, respectively, of a single enlightened source.

All of this is to say that Buddhists, at least Mahayana Buddhists, find little that is objectionable in the notion that Jesus is the manifestation of a deity or the embodiment of a particular quality or attribute like wisdom (*Sophia*) or "the Word" (Logos). Not all Mahayana Buddhists may of course themselves consider Jesus to be such a manifestation, but many will at least accede to the possibility. In any case, that Jesus could at least in theory have emanated from a divine source is within the realm of possibility for those who share the Mahayana worldview. Certainly, the events in the life of Jesus point to the fact that he was an extraordinary individual, and the claim that Jesus is a divine incarnation is as good an explanation as any for his exceptional qualities.

Mahayana Buddhists may thus be quite open to the possibility that Jesus had a divine source and that he therefore shares in the extraordinary status of the deity from which he derived. But as stated earlier, even some mundane deities—deities that have yet to reach the perfected state—have the ability to incarnate physically in the material realm. So the mere fact that Jesus is an incarnation may imply that he is extraordinary, but for Buddhists it does not guarantee that he possesses the quality of maximal greatness. That of course will depend on the nature of the deity that is his source. To identify the deity as the God of the Hebrew Bible, as Christians are wont to do, does not, it seems to me, strengthen the case for Jesus, for that deity seems from all accounts to be far from perfected. The God of the Hebrew Bible is a jealous one that demands the undivided loyalty of its followers, it demands of them blood sacrifice, it is partial and capable of seemingly malevolent actions, to the point of even engaging in violent reprisals against those who refuse to obey its will. Of course, Jesus' appearance in the world is seen by Christians as ushering in a new age, one that reveals a kinder, gentler, more universalistic side to the God of the Hebrew Bible. But the slate of history cannot so easily be wiped clean. Those who would identify Jesus with the God of the Hebrew Bible make him heir to a divine legacy that is, from a Buddhist viewpoint, at the very least of questionable worth.

If the association of Jesus with the historical God of the Hebrew Bible casts moral aspersions on the identity of Jesus, the association of Jesus with the God of later Christian theological speculation represents a different kind of stumbling block for Buddhists: a logical one. I am not referring here to the kinds of logical problems that result from the fact of Christ's dual human/divine nature, problems that also plague Mahayana Buddhist theories of incarnation with their *dharma/rupa-kaya* distinctions. Instead, the logical stumbling block for Buddhists lies in the attributes ascribed to God. Without attempting to give the reasons behind the Buddhist objections, let me simply list here the points of contention. (1) Buddhists repudiate the notion of a creator god, since they maintain that the universe is beginningless. (2) They reject the idea of a being who is primordially pure from beginningless time, since all beings, even enlightened ones, must at one point in time have been fettered in the cycle of suffering and rebirth. (3) They reject the notion of an omnipotent being. (3a) Especially when such a deity is said also to be omnicompassionate, Buddhists see these dual qualities as being contradictory to the existence of suffering in the world (the problem of evil). (3b) More specifically, most Buddhists balk at the idea that any deity is capable of granting liberation to a being who suffers in samsara. Salvation from suffering is earned through the process of self-purification, not bestowed on one as a gift from above. There is no god who is the creator of the universe, who is originally pure and primordially perfected, who is omnipotent and who can will the salvation of beings. Jesus, therefore, cannot be the incarnation of such a God. This of course leaves the Buddhist asking: With what deity is Jesus then to be associated?

This is ultimately a question that Christians will have to answer. Still, this does not preclude Buddhists from offering their own interpretation. On this issue the most charitable alternative a Buddhist could offer is one that identifies Jesus himself as a *nirmanakaya*—that is, as the physical embodiment of an enlightened being. Though effortlessly asserted, however, such a claim has far-reaching implications, the defense of which is not easily dealt with, for, among other things, it leaves unexplained the contradictions between the teachings of Jesus and classical Buddhist doctrines. Of course, there exist hermeneutical mechanisms within Buddhism to deal with such contradictions, to wit, the doctrine of *upaya* or skillful means.[20] But the point still remains: it is necessary to deal in *some way* with the implications of such a claim.

Finally, and briefly, Christians view Jesus' status as a divine incarnation to be a unique event in human history, and this too is problematic for Buddhists. As mentioned above, in Mahayana Buddhist cosmology the universe is believed to be filled with beings that have ontological relationships to one or another of a variety of deities. All such instances are, from one point of view, unique, insofar as each incarnation represents a specific aspect of—and therefore has unique relationship to—a given deity. From this perspective it can of course be said that Jesus' status in this regard is unique, but as a phenomenon in the religious history of the universe, the manifestation of Jesus on the earth is far from the singular event that most Christians believe it to be. This at least is the Buddhist view.

JESUS AS MESSIAH

ONE OF MY most memorable adventures as a cultural intermediary occurred about twelve years ago when I translated for a Christian colleague who was visiting the monastery in southern India where I was living. He was there working on a translation of a Buddhist text, and I volunteered my services as interpreter. One day, in the course of his conversations with one of the senior scholars of the monastery, it came up that he was a Christian, and my teacher asked him to share some of his beliefs. My friend chose to focus on Jesus' identity as messiah. As I finished translating the words of my colleague, my teacher broke out in a fit of laughter, much to my embarrassment. He then proceeded to question his interlocutor in the kind of pointed and unabashedly adversarial way that is typical of the Tibetan monastic debate courtyard. There ensued a lively exchange, but when all was said and done, my teacher's basic question was this: How can the death of one individual act as the direct and substantive cause for the salvation for others?

Behind this interreligious impasse there are of course operative several Buddhist doctrinal presuppositions that are in marked contrast (at times even in opposition) to those of traditional Christianity, not the least of which is the Buddhist vision of what constitutes liberation.[21] Several corollaries to the Buddhist view of liberation are especially relevant as responses to the Christian confession of Jesus as messiah. (1) Each of us is responsible for our own lot in life. We each cause our own suffering, and each of us is ultimately responsible for our own liberation. (2) Our salvation is not dependent on any one historical event. Specifically, our salvation is not dependent upon the appearance of any one personage in history. True, the actions of others can help us or hinder us on the way, but no action (or lack of action) on the part of another individual—whether human or divine—can seal our fate, either as regards salvation or damnation. (3) Soteriologically, there is no end to time, no time after which sentient beings will suffer, and thus long will there be the possibility of their liberation. (4) No being has the capacity to decide whether or not we will be saved. Salvation is not granted to us, or withheld from us, by some external force. It is self-earned. (5) No single action on our part can instantaneously cause our liberation. What brings about salvation is not mere belief or faith, even a faith that is sustained throughout an entire life. Certainly, it is not the instantaneous *belief in something* (e.g., the belief that Jesus is Lord) that brings about salvation, but the long and arduous process of radical mental transformation, which requires more than simply belief.[22]

Together these various tenets make it impossible for Buddhists to accept a messianic creed of the traditional Christian sort. Jesus may have been an extraordinary human being, a sage, an effective and charismatic teacher, and even the manifestation of a deity, but he cannot have been the messiah that most Christians believe him to have been.[23]

CONCLUDING NOTE

IT WILL NOT have gone unnoticed that many of the Buddhist responses to Jesus presented in this essay have strong affinities to positions found in Christian Gnosticism. What historical links, if any, exist between Buddhism and Gnosticism remains for the most part an unresolved scholarly issue. That there do exist such links at least in the realm of ideas, however, can hardly be denied, and perhaps this is as good a time as any to suggest that such commonalities of perspective deserve greater scholarly attention. At the same time, despite the similarities, it is clearly too facile to simply equate Buddhism with Gnosticism, as Pope John Paul II does for clearly polemical purposes in a recent book.[24]

The value of the above remarks—to the extent that they have any—may lie principally in the fact that they provide Christians with a perspective on

Jesus that is foreign and therefore fresh. If, in the process, they also manage to evoke the memory of a more familiar but forgotten voice, that of Christian Gnosticism, perhaps this is an overtone to the discussion that is not unwanted, adding as it does a third—albeit more muted—voice to the dialogue; and that, it seems to me, can only add to its richness.

Notes

1. For more on what is perhaps a nonstandard use of the word *theology* and on what I take the academic Buddhist theological task to be, see my forthcoming "Buddhist Theology in the Academy," in Roger R. Jackson and John J. Makransky, eds., *Buddhist Theology* (London: Curzon Press), Critical Studies in Buddhism Series.

2. My views of buddhology as an academic discipline can be gleaned from my "Buddhist Studies as a Discipline and the Role of Theory," *Journal of the International Association of Buddhist Studies* 18, no. 2 (1995), pp. 231–68.

3. We call ourselves the "Buddhist-Christian Contemplative Service" and we have met since 1995 at St. Paul's United Methodist Church in Denver. I am cofounder of the group together with Rev. Toni Cook (an ordained United Methodist minister) and Sister Mary Luke Tobin (a Catholic sister of Loretto).

4. John Dominic Crossan, *The Historical Jesus: The Life of a Mediterranean Jewish Peasant* (San Francisco: HarperSanFrancisco, 1991).

5. Sheila Greeve Davaney, "A Historicist Model for Theology," in Jeffrey Carlson and Robert A. Ludwig, eds., *Jesus and Faith: A Conversation on the Work of John Dominic Crossan, Author of* The Historical Jesus (Maryknoll, New York: Orbis Books, 1994), p. 50.

6. John Dominic Crossan, "The Historical Jesus in Early Christianity" in Jeffrey Carlson and Robert A. Ludwig, eds., *Jesus and Faith: A Conversation on the Work of John Dominic Crossan, Author of* The Historical Jesus (Maryknoll, New York: Orbis Books, 1994), p. 3.

7. This is true despite the attempts by some scholars to imply a greater similarity between the reformist traditions of the two figures. See, for example, the discussion of the work of the anthropologist James C. Scott in Crossan, ibid., p. 2.

8. Especially on the latter point, see Christopher S. Queen and Sally B. King, eds., *Engaged Buddhism: Buddhist Liberation Movements in Asia* (Albany: State University of New York Press, 1996). My own essay in that volume actually contrasts one such Buddhist movement (the Dalai Lama's Tibetan independence movement) with Latin American liberation theology.

9. I base the fact that there is relative consensus on the passages cited below on the results of the work of the Jesus Seminar; see Robert W. Funk, Roy W. Hoover, and the Jesus Seminar, *The Five Gospels: The Search for the Authentic Words of Jesus* (New York: Scribner, 1993).

10. Space does not permit me to go into any detail concerning why this portion of the Gospel of Matthew appeals so to Buddhists. Instead I refer readers to the Dalai Lama's recent commentary on this (and other) portions of the New Testament; see his *The Good Heart: A Buddhist Perspective on the Teachings of Jesus* (Boston: Wisdom, 1996).

11. Marcus Borg characterizes Jesus as a teacher of subversive wisdom. Jesus' teachings, he says, "are crystallizations of insight which, either radical in themselves or radical in their application, frequently embody the theme of world reversal. They are invitations to see differently, bringing about a shattering of world." Such a "Zen-master Jesus" is certainly appealing to Buddhists, although I must admit that it is not the picture of Jesus that has ever come to my mind as I have read through the gospels. But even if what Borg says is accurate, it seems to me that several observations are in order. (1) Jesus, as far as I can tell, does not have this picture of himself. For example, he does not, to my knowledge, ever speak of the insight- or wisdom-generating function of his teachings. (2) This does not of course imply that Jesus cannot be so interpreted retrospectively, as it were, regardless of Jesus' own self-image. But to the extent that Jesus' teachings can be interpreted as koan-like vehicles for world-shattering, it seems to me that the emphasis must still be placed on the term *world,* for the function of these teachings seems to be social rather than personal transformation. (3) Perhaps this dichotomy is not altogether appropriate, however, for Borg's point in part is that such a program of social transformation is brought about precisely by the personal transformation wrought by Jesus' teachings. This is certainly a welcomed perspective from a Buddhist point of view, although I believe that it still leaves Buddhists with questions about Jesus' vision of the nature of salvation and with a hankering for more explicit details on the exact relationship of wisdom to salvation.

12. By suggesting that the Gnostic material contains parallels to Buddhism, I do not wish to imply a simple identity between the two traditions. There are of course clear differences. For example, the portrayal of the material world as evil in a great deal of Gnostic literature is anathema to Buddhists.

13. In the Indo-Tibetan tradition, for example, the Kalacakra tantra espouses a kind of apocalypticism when it speaks of a great war giving way to an eight-hundred-year period during which the teachings of Buddhism will flourish. See Helmut Hoffman, *The Religions of Tibet* (trans. Edward Fitzgerald), (London: Allen and Unwin, 1961), pp. 125–26; and Tenzin Gyatso, the Dalai Lama, and Jeffrey Hopkins, *Kalacakra Tantra: Rite of Initiation* (London: Wisdom, 2nd ed. 1989), p. 65.

14. I am not unaware of the fact that recent scholarship on Jesus has brought about what Borg calls "the collapse of the eschatological Jesus"; Marcus Borg, ibid., p. 13. Nonetheless, it can hardly be denied that the end-of-time interpretation of Jesus' "Kingdom of God" teachings has been at the very least central to Christianity. What is more, it remains unclear to me how those teachings are to be explained if not in an eschatological fashion, and perhaps this is a point that the Christian respondents in this volume could elucidate.

15. On the distinction between mundane and supramundane deities, see Rene de Nebesky-Wojkowitz, *Oracles and Demons of Tibet: The Cult and Iconography of Tibetan Protective Deities* (Taipei: SMC, reprint of the 1956 ed.), pp. 3–5.

16. The ability to manifest different physical forms is not limited to nonphysical deities. Even humans can accomplish this as the result of certain meditative exercises. This is one of several extraordinary achievements spoken of as being the fruit of meditative practice. See, for example, the discussion of the *iddhis* (especially the first and third *iddhis*) in *Visuddhimagga* (XII, 23–25), trans. Bhikkhu Nanamoli (Kandy: Buddhist Publication Society, 1991), p. 374; and also Paravahera vajirajnana Mahathera, *Buddhist Meditation in Theory and Practice* (Kuala Lumpur: Buddhist Missionary Society, 1975), pp. 425–26.

17. The most extensive treatment of the *buddhakayas* in a Western language is John J. Makransky, *Buddhahood Embodied: Sources of Controversy in India and Tibet* (Albany: State University of New York Press, 1997), see especially chapter 5.

18. "Manjusri, the epitome of the conqueror's wisdom;" tib. *Rgyal ba'i mkhyen rab kun 'dus 'jam dpal dbyangs*. A line from a well-known Tibetan prayer; in *Daily Recitation of Preliminaries* (Dharamsala: Library of Tibetan Works and Archives, 1975), p. 5.

19. For a more complete treatment of Buddhist objections to the traditional God of Christian theology, see Gunapala Dharmasiri, *A Buddhist Critique of the Christian concept of God* (Kandy: Lake House Investments, 1974); and also Roger R. Jackson, "Dharmakirti's Refutation of Theism," *Philosophy East and West* 36, no. 4 (1986), pp. 315–48.

20. On this doctrine as a hermeneutical device, see my *Buddhism and Language: A Study of Indo-Tibetan Scholasticism* (Albany: State University of New York Press, 1994), especially chapter 3.

21. See my "Liberation: An Indo-Tibetan Perspective," and response to Terry C. Muck, in *Buddhist-Christian Studies*, 1993.

22. I am not unaware of the fact that in the history of Buddhism there have been movements that challenge this notion of the nature and path to salvation. Especially important to mention in this regard are certain schools of Japanese Pure Land Buddhism. But again, I remind my readers that I am speaking here principally from an Indo-Tibetan Buddhist doctrinal perspective.

23. Of course, if the Jesus Seminar is right, then Jesus did not make this claim of himself. See Funk et. al, *The Five Gospels*, pp. 32–34.

24. For a response to the Pope's polemic against Buddhism, see my essay, "A Buddhist Response to H. H., John Paul II," in Harold Kasimow and Byron Sherwin, eds., *No faith Is an Island: John Paul II and Interreligious Dialogue* (Maryknoll, New York: Orbis Books, forthcoming).

Meditating on Jesus

RITA M. GROSS

University of Wisconsin–Eau Claire

THE TOPIC[1] OF developing a Buddhist view of Jesus is challenging to me on many levels, for many reasons. Not the least of them involves my own unhappy childhood and young adulthood being trained as a member of a version of Christianity that expressed an extremely exclusivist position regarding religious pluralism. Nevertheless, I have long practiced Buddhist-Christian dialogue as a Buddhist, in part as an antidote to that unhappy past, as a deliberate attempt to heal the wounds inflicted on me by an exclusivist and doctrinaire version of Christianity. So why does this task of developing a Buddhist view of Jesus remain difficult?

In part this task is difficult because it is unfamiliar. In my world religions classes, I routinely present Jewish views of Jesus, but there is little reason to discuss Jesus in the perspectives of other major religions and I have almost never broached the topic. In my feminist theology classes, I again discuss feminist reactions to Jesus, but there is little reason to present a feminist Buddhist perspective on Jesus. Little Buddhist literature about Buddhist reactions to Jesus and few Buddhist assessments of Christianity exist, though the reverse is not true,[2] which perhaps indicates that fellow Buddhists have also felt little need to develop a reaction to or a position about Jesus. But it is also difficult because in Buddhist-Christian dialogue, we often discuss more abstract and less troublesome topics than the traditional Christian evaluation of Jesus, with its undeniably exclusivistic and universal truth claims. Thus, in many ways, I have been able to keep a distance between my own experiences of Christianity and my own experiences of Buddhism. Encountering Christians in Buddhist-Christian dialogue and teaching Christian feminist theology are really much simpler than trying to untangle my own Buddhist reactions to central Christian claims, including especially claims about the ultimate and universal significance of Jesus.

Nevertheless, it is clear that my task in this essay is to react to Jesus as a Buddhist, something I have not done formally in any other context. Therefore, I have proceeded with the assumption that my task is to find the relevant Buddhist categories for interpreting Jesus in Buddhist terms, to delineate them briefly to non-Buddhists, and then to apply them to Jesus or to Christian claims about Jesus. This assignment is not as innocent or as easy as it seems at first reading. The first difficulty is determining who or what one is reacting to in the exercise of developing a Buddhist view of Jesus. Depending on who or what one understands Jesus to be, or depending on which Christian claims about Jesus one comments upon, a Buddhist could have radically different views about Jesus. So clearly, the first task in developing a Buddhist view of Jesus is to determine which Jesus will be discussed. Then, secondly, it is difficult but important to maintain the primary focus as a Buddhist focus, using Buddhist rather than Christian categories to control the discourse. I say this because much of the literature seems to compare Buddhism to Christianity, placing Christianity and Christian categories in central focus and matching concepts from the Christian point of view. I want to match concepts with Buddhist categories as my central reference point, fitting the Christian Jesus into a Buddhist framework.

How should I, as a Buddhist, determine what is meant by the Christian category *Jesus?* As is evidenced by the radically different images of Jesus in popular Christianity, by much recent scholarship on the gospels, and by a diverse body of Christological writings, Christians themselves would be hard pressed to give a definitive or a short answer to the question "Just who or what am I supposed to be discussing from a Buddhist point of view?" Am I to talk of the historical Jesus, of the Jesus of the gospels, of the Jesus of the early church, or of Jesus as understood through central theological doctrines, such as Trinity and Incarnation, which are actually much later in their genesis? My assignment, which is to discuss "the Jesus of Christianity,"[3] does not really solve that problem, since there are so many Jesuses of Christianity. But I think we can safely assume that "the Jesus of Christianity" includes all the above *except,* perhaps, the historical Jesus, who is a recent construction and not so central to many Christians' religious lives. In any case, I shall direct most of my comments to Jesus as he has been interpreted by major stands within Christianity and will not try to solve the problem of whether he ever intended to leave such a message or what his own intended message may have been.

With that decision, we invite some ghosts to enter. Christianity is not only something I learned about academically or at a distance, as would be the case for most Buddhists. Rather, as already said, my early indoctrination involved an extremely exclusivist interpretation of Jesus. Experientially, for me, the central Christian claim about Jesus is the exclusivist interpretation of belief in Jesus' redemptive death and resurrection as the only way to "salvation." Though I know intellectually that inclusivist and pluralist Christian views of Jesus are well developed, nevertheless, to me they do not seem to carry the normative and traditional weight that the exclusivist position carries. And exclusivist truth claims in religion, I would argue, are among the most dangerous, destructive, and immoral ideas that humans have ever created.

Therefore, for me, the first hurdle that must be negotiated in developing a Buddhist view of Jesus is the hurdle of exclusive truth claims, which involves developing a philosophy of religious pluralism, based on Buddhist categories, that is radically nonexclusivist. This task is so central for me because of the way in which I left the only kind of Christianity I knew experientially. Though I was, and still am, quite sincere in my spiritual inclinations and quite capable of understanding abstract theological concepts, I was also "too thoughtful" and "asked too many questions," as it was put to me. During my senior year of college, I was excommunicated for heresy and confidently told that I would go to hell for my religious views. The major bone of contention was my view of religious pluralism, namely that people of all religions "could be saved," as I naively put it in those days before I had studied much comparative religion. I had been indoctrinated that all non-Christian religions and most other versions of Christianity were "false." Ridicule of these other beliefs, pity for people misguided and deluded into adherence to such folly, and devotion to the cause of converting them to "the one true faith" were daily fare. Obviously, the exclusive claims made on behalf of Jesus by Christians appalled me even as a teenager, and my repugnance for exclusive truth claims on the part of religions—any religion—has not diminished since. Thus, part of my journey is working out both a theory and a praxis of religious pluralism that is neither relativistic nor universalistic, that encourages both commitment to one tradition and appreciation of other traditions.

I am aware that currently most liberal Christian theologians are as appalled by this tradition of exclusivism as I am. I am also aware that the World Council of Churches and the Roman Catholic Church, in Vatican II, have come to a position on religious pluralism that is often called the "inclusivist position," which is claimed to diverge sharply from the exclusivist position. The inclusivist position "affirm[s] the value and dignity of all religious paths." Nevertheless, this position, like the exclusivist position, "attributes to Christ and Christianity . . . an ultimacy and normativity meant to embrace and fulfill all other religions." Additionally, according to Paul Knitter, inclusivist Christians also "interpret the uniqueness of Jesus in terms of finality and unsurpassability."[4] As a Buddhist, I find these claims offensive, and I think most non-Christians probably share my reaction. Nor would I feel comfortable, as a Buddhist, in making the same claim about Buddhism vis-à-vis Christianity.

I am also aware of an even newer and smaller voice in Christian theology called the "pluralist" position. I have much more sympathy with this position, which claims a "*possible* parity of all religions and . . . eschew[s] any final or absolute truth." What I am not in sympathy with is their claim, at least as expressed by Paul Knitter, that "Jesus' uniqueness [is] the *universality* and *indispensability* of His message and mission."[5] My objections are fairly subtle; this claim seems to state both that Jesus is unique among religious figures and that he had a message and a mission that the world cannot do without, for I see no other way to read the words *universal* and *indispensable* in Paul Knitter's statement. As a Buddhist, I'm not at all sure that I see Jesus as unique, as universal, or as indispensable, which makes me question this version of Christian pluralism. I realize that as a Buddhist I probably often feel and sound the same way about the message and mission of Buddhism that Paul Knitter sounds about the message and mission of Jesus. But I try to regard that tone in my rhetoric as a failing rather than a virtue. Such assessments of Buddhism are so demeaning to non-Buddhists.

These two recent Christian attempts to disown the dominant doctrines throughout most of Christian history cannot, for me, undo the emotional damage done by exclusivist indoctrination, atone for the historical record of inhumane acts and attitudes motivated by exclusivist attitudes, or counter my impression that most of my Christian students and neighbors are not inclusivists or pluralists. True, the person in the street usually is rather unfamiliar with the depth dimension of his or her religion and is probably a rather poor spokesperson for it. Buddhist popular religion is not especially edifying either. However, I object to the Jesus of popular religion as interpreted by major strands of Christianity not because this interpretation is unedifying or crude, but because this very widespread and prevalent interpretation is *dangerous, destructive, and degraded.* The impact of the Jesus of Christianity on people in other world religions has often been quite negative. The gap between the esoteric Jesus of nonexclusivists and the exoteric universal and indispensable savior whom all must confess and often are compelled to confess is enormous. I will speak, admittedly prompted by ghosts of confirmation classes past, to this more familiar Jesus found in the rhetoric of many, many Christians.

Some have criticized me throughout the years for not regarding the conservative sect in which I was raised, with its strongly exclusivist position, as an aberrant and degraded form of Christianity. Such critics argue that I could have found another version of Christianity that would have been less given to such exaggerations. I am also told that my assessments of Christianity are not accurate because they are too colored by my experiences with an extreme position. Unfortunately, whether correctly or incorrectly, I cannot see this sect as so completely aberrant a form of Christianity, but only as an extremely vociferous exponent of a common position. Most other Christians are not so sure about who will populate heaven and hell as were the members of this sect, but exclusivism and absolutism are entailed by the central claims made about Jesus, as interpreted by large segments of Christianity throughout most of Christian history. And, in spite of the presence of inclusivist and pluralist Christian thought, many of the Christians I encounter are still taught the exclusivist position by their churches and are completely unaware of other Christian positions on religious pluralism. Every semester, I encounter students who have been indoctrinated to such positions very recently. For example, my Catholic students all know that Catholics are not supposed to use birth control, but few of them know that Vatican II recommends a somewhat inclusivist view of religious pluralism. Since religious exclusivism is much more dangerous and has caused a great deal more pain than has the practice of birth control, one would think that educating Catholics about their church's contemporary position on religious pluralism would be a higher priority.

This train of reasoning, whether correct or incorrect, keeps me, as an act of prophetic faithfulness, from adhering to a religion for which absolute and exclusive truth claims are or have been central and which, therefore, has a poor historical record of dealing with religious pluralism and coexistence. That is why I could not become a liberal Christian. That is also why I continue to focus on alternatives to religious exclusivism as the heart of my Buddhist view of Jesus.

Religious Language and Religious Pluralism

Since religions make verbal statements that are frequently taken as accurate assessments of ultimate reality by their adherents, it might be wondered how any religion could avoid absolutism and exclusivism. It might further be wondered if I could, without violating my own pluralistic principles, adhere to Buddhism, since Buddhism, like Christianity, is one of the few religions that even tries to promote itself to outsiders. I want to try to deal with these very reasonable questions by talking about the Buddhist attitude toward verbal and conceptual formulations of truth, which I find highly attractive precisely because it seems to me to allow a position that is neither relativistic nor exclusivistic.

Regarding the purpose of doctrinal statements, in my view Buddhism and Christianity differ sharply. I have not found a more succinct or accurate summary of the Buddhist position than that of Paul Griffiths: "[T]here is a methodological principle . . . that has to do with the nature of religious doctrines. Briefly and rather crudely, this principle suggests that religious doctrines have utility rather than truth; that their importance lies in the effects they have upon those who believe in them."[6] Space does not permit me to demonstrate that this is indeed the Buddhist position, but let us assume that Griffiths is correct.

In Buddhist terms, this means that verbal doctrines are ultimately in the realm of *upaya,* skillful means or method, not the realm of *prajna,* intuitive clear seeing or "truth."[7] This is an extremely fruitful insight, for Buddhism, like Christianity, would affirm that *prajna* is unitive and the same for all people in all cases. But truth is not a matter of doctrines and doctrines are neither true nor false; they are more or less useful in the circumstances at hand. Truth, or *prajna* (literally, "superior knowledge"), has always been understood more as ability than as a body of information, more as "knowing" than as "knowledge" in Buddhism. It can be hinted at and pointed to, but even the finest doctrine is merely a pointer. Nothing makes this point more forcefully than the famous "raft parable" attributed to the Buddha. "Oh Bhikkhus, even this view, which is so pure and so clear, if you cling to it, if you fondle it, if you treasure it, then you do not understand that the teaching is similar to a raft, which is for crossing over, and not for getting hold of."[8] Truth is extra-verbal and verbal formulations of truth are approximations, not final statements.

On the other hand, *upaya,* usually translated as "skillful means" or "method," has always been understood to be multiple, even infinitely various, because what is crucial is finding the method or tool *appropriate to the circumstances* at hand. The more skilled the interpreter or teacher of Buddhism, the greater his or her repertoire of appropriate skillful means. No one would be so foolish as to expect to find a tool that works for every task and, therefore, one should not attempt to find a one-size-fits-all doctrine. One would be foolish to universalize or absolutize a doctrine or to claim that only adherents of this doctrine are adequate spiritually.

The point that doctrine is in the realm of *upaya* rather than the realm of *prajna* is important and subtle because westerners are extremely likely to miss it as a result of their cultural training and preconceptions. First of all, neither the distinction between method and truth nor the claims that they are of coequal importance is part of the Western frame of discourse. Second, if the distinction were even recognized, westerners would be likely to regard *prajna* as "real"—really true—while *upaya* would be regarded as secondary and approximate. In the many years that I have spent trying to assimilate genuinely Buddhist modes of apprehension, nothing has been more foreign than the coequal status of *prajna* with *upaya* or the relegation of verbal truths to the realm of *upaya*. Thus I find these conceptual possibilities to be a genuine relief and a way out of absolutist modes of discourse that I had found unbearable.

Though again space does not permit a demonstration, I think the mainline traditional Christian view is quite the opposite. Doctrines may contain utility, but their most important function is their truth value as is evidenced by the longstanding concern with what people will confess verbally. There is a close link between words and truth in many Christian assessments and more trust that words can convey truth than is typical of most other religions. Therefore, verbal doctrines are primarily evaluated as true or false, not as salutary or destructive. This method fuels the hope for, and often the claim of, final truth in verbal form. As a result, Christians, more than most other religious traditions, try to distill true doctrine into a succinct creed and often regard adherence to that creed as more important than understanding of it. Confession of those verbal doctrines matters ultimately. Hence, these doctrines are easily absolutized by claiming exclusive truth for them, and nonadherents are easily regarded as inferior.

To regard doctrines as more important and worthwhile for their verbal utility than for their verbal truth and to judge them more by their effects on adherents than by their verbal contents seems to me to overcome absolutism with all its attendant problems while not falling into relativism. First of all, with this attitude, one does not have to absolutize one's own concepts of truth nor to long for a world in which all agree on the same expressions of truth. Rather, religious symbol systems could coexist and complement each other like colors of a rainbow.[9] A religious myth or symbol would be regarded as a poem rather than as a historical or scientific statement. I would argue that most exclusive truth claims in religion are based on regarding religion as more akin to what westerners now call "history" or "science" than what westerners now call "art" or "poetry." Superficially, many people think that the question in historical or scientific disciplines is the question of truth or falsity, while the question for art, poetry, or mythology is a question of taste or aesthetics. Generally, people are much more flexible and nonexclusive about aesthetic judgments than about historical or scientific claims. No one would want to abolish all poetry in the world except for one's favorite poem, nor even expect everyone to agree that this is the most wonderful poem ever written. Why should it be different with religious doctrines, which are ultimately mythopoeic, not discursive, in their mode of discourse? Ironically, such an attitude would also make religious statements more rather than less like scientific or historical statements, because those who understand these disciplines realize that scientific and historical statements are hypotheses, subject to a continual process of change, adjustment, and refinement, not some final and absolute statement. No sensible person is ever more than provisionally committed to a hypothesis, which does not lessen its force to explain or motivate in the absence of a better hypothesis. With the world's religions, we have a number of reasonably cogent hypotheses about some rather unanswerable questions. The myth and symbol system surrounding Jesus could well be one such hypothesis, but that has not been a mainstream understanding of the Jesus of Christianity.

One who judges a doctrine on the basis of what it does rather than on its literal or verbal truth value also has another excellent basis for appreciating a foreign symbol system that is conceptually incompatible with one's own. It can be appreciated not only as a wonderful poem and an interesting hypothesis, but as a source of humane behavior in the world. Such is the basis for the Dalai Lama's encomiums of Christianity in his frequent pleas for tolerance, mutual respect, and coexistence among the world's religions: "Through the various religious systems, followers are assuming a salutary attitude toward their fellow human beings—our brothers and sisters—and implementing this good motivation in the service of human society. This has been demonstrated by a great many believers in Christianity throughout history. Many have sacrificed their lives for the benefit of humankind."[10] This statement is made despite major doctrinal differences between Buddhism and Christianity—of which the Dalai Lama is well aware—and his own personal devotion to the Buddhist symbols and doctrines.

At the same time, assessing doctrines on their utility means that the charge of relativism, often brought against pluralists, is countered. While, in general, relativism seems superior to absolutism because it is more humane and less ethnocentric, logic compels one to admit that there must be limits to relativism. Finding that boundary is never easy. But clearly, any doctrine that encourages intolerance and mutual hostility would be negatively evaluated, using the criterion of utility. Most doctrines do not, in and of themselves, engender mutual disrespect and hostility, *unless they are absolutized.* And almost any doctrine, whatever its contents, could then be utilized inhumanely if it is absolutized. Thus at least one limit to relativism would be the absolutizing of any doctrine or any doctrine that cannot be de-absolutized by the very nature of its claims. Such doctrines, because of their exclusivism and absolutism, cannot claim parity or equal validity with other doctrines that do not seek such a monopoly on religious expression. (Is monotheism the prime example of such a claim?) Pluralism and doctrines that are absolutized cannot coexist. Given the frequent and widespread negative results of absolutism, it seems clear that, using the method of judging doctrines on their utility, this impasse can be resolved morally only by renouncing doctrinal absolutism. Probably conventional Christian claims about Jesus fall under judgment of being a conceptual absolute. I also feel quite certain that the Jesus myth does not have to be subjected to such absolutisms.

Sometimes when I argue in this fashion, people accuse me of merely substituting one absolute—pluralism—for another. But they misunderstand, for I am suggesting a *methodological* absolute, not a doctrinal absolute. There is every difference in the world between a methodological absolute and a doctrinal absolute. This methodological absolute—that doctrines should be evaluated on the basis of their effect on behavior, not their verbal truth value—definitively undercuts any attempt to establish a doctrinal or ideological absolute. Precisely this is what is required in the world, at least at present. Furthermore, we also notice that the methodological absolute of evaluating doctrines on the basis of their utility allows us to posit *ethical* absolutes, such as nonharming, even though conceptual or doctrinal absolutes are impossible.

If we reflect further, we also notice that despite glaring oppositions at the level of symbol and doctrine, the world's major religions have all produced a remarkably similar core basic ethic. We also must notice that, unfortunately, they have produced remarkably similar ethical distortions as well, of which patriarchal sexism is one of the more widespread and serious. This should indicate that no major doctrinal system is so far off the mark that it cannot produce a relevant ethic, nor so perfect that it guards its adherents against ethical failure. It should also indicate that the specific symbol, myth, and doctrines of choice are not all that central and that the more urgent realm for ultimate concern is our interactions with our world, not our modes of symbolizing or theorizing that world.

Thus it is clear that I am neither advocating mere relativism nor merely substituting one absolute for another. I am advocating *conceptual* relativism along with minimal *moral* and *methodological* absolutes. Because absolutes can be so dangerous, they should always be kept to the barest possible minimum, but sheer relativism is equally dangerous. To refrain from conceptual and doctrinal absolutes while giving one's loyalty and energy to ethical and methodological absolutes is the appropriate negotiation of that difficult passage.

Finally, I want as a Buddhist to react to the evaluation of some Christian pluralists who, while they do not absolutize the Jesus of Christianity, nevertheless posit an "indispensability and uniqueness" for his message and mission. Such rhetoric pressures non-Christians at least to think Jesus was an extraordinary, extremely incredible human being, even if they don't agree with Christological doctrines. Many, even members of groups that have not been treated well historically by Christians, such as Jews or feminists, politely make the case that Jesus was really okay—it's what Christians have done to him that's the problem. Such rhetoric is, I believe, a concession to Christian pressure to venerate Jesus even if one does not worship him.

I have questioned whether such Christians take the time to do a basic exercise in empathy in which they would imagine how such claims come across to non-Christians. Returning for a moment to the criterion of utility as a norm for judging concepts, such claims seem to me to be seriously lacking in *upaya*, or skillful methods, because of their negative effects on listeners such as myself. To me they certainly are not attractive, and I feel an unwelcome pressure to revere Jesus as someone whom I find unique and indispensable, which is not the case. For me, emotionally, when Christians insist that Jesus must be seen as indispensable and universal in his message and mission, it becomes almost impossible to appreciate him in any way at any level. Such rhetoric pushes me to the opposite reaction: "Why should I?" I would prefer to be allowed to have no opinion, to be neutral and agnostic regarding the uniqueness and indispensability of Jesus' mission and message.

The Christian pluralist's claims for the indispensability and uniqueness of his message and mission put me in the unwelcome position of having to explain why I cannot share that judgment even though I do not wish to disparage Jesus any more than I wish to venerate or praise him. I am serious when I say that I can see no basis for venerating Jesus as a human being in a league by himself unsurpassed or unequaled by other human beings in his heroism, compassion, wisdom, or godliness, or in the cogency and relevance of his message. I can't get that extreme of uniqueness out of my reading of the New Testament.

I suspect that many conservative Christians might, in a roundabout way, agree with me. Humanist and rationalist Christians often emphasize the human Jesus as a uniquely impressive human being. The more traditional Christian reason to see Jesus as unique is to state that he is "the only begotten son of God." This separates him from all other human beings, whose task is to worship, rather than to venerate him. And his task is to do what no human can do—to atone for sin and redeem humanity. This way of understanding Jesus emphasizes the mission over the message and sees Jesus as external savior who confers or bestows liberation on another. In Buddhist terms, this is the essence of theism, the most puzzling and unrealistic doctrine of Christianity to a Buddhist. At this point, as a Buddhist, I simply pull back to listen.

A Buddhist Jesus

But setting aside claims at any level, whether absolute or relative, as to the uniqueness and indispensability of Jesus' message and mission, how could a Buddhist fit Jesus into a Buddhist framework? In listening to comparisons of the Buddha and the Christ, I have often been struck by the impression that, because of the political hegemony of Western thought modes, most of the discourse regards the Jesus of Christianity as the normative figure and tries to understand the Buddha in his terms, by comparison with him. I want to reverse that process and try to explore what a genuinely Buddhist Jesus might be like.

This process begins by noting a less serious—though perhaps more interesting—difference between Buddhism and Christianity than Christian claims about the uniqueness and indispensability of the message and mission of

Jesus. The Christian tendency is to locate truth in the messenger, whereas Buddhism tends to focus on the message. This I think correlates well the Christian tendency to personify the ultimate while Buddhists tend toward nonpersonal metaphors about ultimate reality. I cannot think of any reason to argue that one style is more conducive to humane behavior than the other, so using the principle of assessing doctrines on the basis of their utility, I see no reason to draw these two styles into competition with each other. Because I regard absolutism and exclusivism as the problem, I would not critique the Christian tendency to center on the messenger, but its tendency to absolutize the Messenger.

Though Buddhism does not focus on the messenger, nevertheless it has developed a considerable repertoire of anthropomorphic and personalized symbols that can be of considerable significance on the spiritual path of the Buddhist. Using the method of mutual transformation through dialogue, I want to suggest that Christians seeking ways to go beyond absolutizing the Messenger might well study Buddhist ways of mythologizing and conceptualizing their personal and anthropomorphic figures, which are important and spiritually helpful, but are not absolutized. Therefore, I will indulge in a constructive fantasy, imagining how I would see Jesus interpreted if Buddhist ways of interpreting the messenger were to be utilized by Christians.

This exercise should be grounded in several generalizations about anthropomorphic figures in Buddhism. First, in every case, there are numerous examples of each type. No one is ultimately unique, though each has ordinary uniqueness—that is to say, individuality. Second, they are always human examples and ideals, not lords of an unattainable state. They are exalted and may be far beyond my current abilities, but not beyond my human capabilities. Thus, we approach them with veneration but not with worship. This distinction between worship and veneration is critical for explaining the difference in attitude and ritual mood between nontheism and theism—and often between Asian and monotheistic forms of religion. Veneration honors and respects someone who has attained a great deal and inspires the venerator to strive toward that attainment, but there is no metaphysical duality between venerator and venerated. Worship declares allegiance and praises or thanks the other, acknowledging an ultimate duality between worshiper and worshiped.

When discussing important anthropomorphic symbols in Buddhism and comparing them to the Jesus of Christianity, the first figure that comes to mind is, of course, the Buddha figure. Hence, Christians who wish to draw parallels between Jesus and other important religious figures often suggest this comparison. After all, both the Buddha and Jesus are seen as founders. Buddhists, however, are more likely to compare the Jesus of Christianity with the bodhisattva figure. I share that judgment because classically, rather different claims are made about the Buddha than about Jesus, their biographies are only superficially similar, and their missions are quite different. That both are seen by historians as founders of a new religion is too superficial to create a profound similarity. I doubt that either saw himself as founder of a new religion, nor do their followers regard their religions as nonexistent before the Buddha or Jesus lived.

The major difference between a Buddha and the Christ, which causes these two figures to be quite dissimilar, concerns what their followers believe each can do for the faithful. Buddhists go for refuge to the Buddha as example, but the Buddha's own enlightenment solves only his problems, not theirs. Vicarious enlightenment is not possible according to Buddhist analysis (except for Pure Land Buddhism). Christians have faith in Jesus as the redeemer, whose sacrificial death does what they cannot do, providing the means for reconciliation with a transcendent deity by vicariously atoning for all sin. Vicarious atonement and redemption are the only possibility in classical Christianity.

From this vast difference in declaring whether or not the primary task of the founder is to vicariously save or free the faithful follow other important differences. There is only one Jesus of Christianity, whereas all forms of Buddhism, including those that claim there is only one Buddha in each world age, affirm the existence of multiple Buddhas, the Buddhas of the three times. These Buddhas are more identical than unique; they are difficult to distinguish iconographically and the salient points of their mythic biographies are identical. The point being made is that, wondrous as are the accomplishments of a Buddha, they are not unreduplicatable. The extent to which a Buddhist is encouraged to strive for Buddhahood differs considerably among the various strands of Buddhism, but that others besides Siddartha Gautama become Buddhas is affirmed by all forms of Buddhism, and none claims that Siddartha's Buddhahood saves anyone else.

All forms of Buddhism also mention in passing a little-known figure, the *pratyekabuddha,* often translated as a "solitary Buddha." The meaning of his or her solitariness is that this person understands fully and becomes enlightened without a teacher, simply by deducing the spiritual and physical laws of existence through contemplation. This person not only is not a student of another, but also, unlike a Buddha, does not teach. For this reason, the *pratyekabuddha* is not dwelt upon or honored in most forms of Buddhism. But the importance for a comparison with the Jesus of Christianity is the Buddhist affirmation, again, that salvation need not be mediated by another and that the enlightenment of a Buddha is not unique.

Given Buddhism and Christianity as they are currently constituted, Jesus is not very similar to either a Buddha or a *pratyekabuddha.* Furthermore, the dissimilarities mirror the major doctrinal differences between the two religions. When we discuss the Buddhist bodhisattva figure, however, we find that real similarities exist between the two religions in their current forms. The bodhisattva is known to all forms of Buddhism but is much more central to Mahayana than to Theravadin forms of Buddhism. Not by definition, but by derived implication, a bodhisattva is a future Buddha, someone who has taken the vow to achieve complete perfect unsurpassable enlightenment for the benefit of all sentient beings, rather than to rest with the individually salvific enlightenment of an *arahant.* In Mahayana Buddhism, this is the ideal of all serious adherents of the religion and most take the bodhisattva vow. Those with a casual knowledge of Buddhism often are more familiar with the great mythic bodhisattvas of the Mahayana pantheon, but to emphasize them to the exclusion of the ordinary mundane bodhisattva is incorrect. For one who takes the bodhisattva vow, the emphasis is generally not on the ultimate goal of final enlightenment, but on the intermediate lives of the bodhisattva, who trains ceaselessly in wisdom and method (*prajna* and *upaya* of the first section of this paper), and who is willing to go to any lengths or make any sacrifice that would help others progress spiritually.

Some obvious parallels can be made with the Jesus of Christianity. In Buddhist terms, Jesus seems much more like a bodhisattva than like a Buddha to me. This is because of his willingness to suffer on behalf of others and the extent to which, according to the text itself as well as all forms of Christianity, he put the well-being of others before his own comfort—an important, emotionally moving ideal for Mahayanists. Also, insofar as the imitation of Christ is an important moral ideal in Christianity, the individual Christian's attempt to be Christlike is similar to the Mahayanist's assumption of the bodhisattva's task. This comparison also downplays some of the contrasts that make the comparison of Jesus and Buddha less apt. In both cases, the emphasis is on the passion of the compassionate helper, not on the eventual achievement or results of that passion, which, as we have seen, are quite different.

In Buddhism, it is even clearer that there are many bodhisattvas than it is that the Buddha is not unique. Thus it is easy for a Buddhist to see Jesus as a bodhisattva, as there is no dogma or assumption that all bodhisattvas belong to the Buddhist religion. Since a Buddhist would not say "the bodhisattva," implying that there is only one unique bodhisattva, a Buddhist could easily see Jesus as a bodhisattva without acknowledging Christian claims about his uniqueness or universality. In sum, this is a way that Buddhists can appreciate Jesus in Buddhist terms with a minimum of conflict between Buddhist assertions and Christian assertions. Probably, however, even the Christian pluralist wouldn't be satisfied, since a Buddhist *could,* if she or he wanted, venerate Jesus as a bodhisattva, but no Buddhist would claim that one *must* venerate *this* bodhisattva, or insist on "the universality and indispensability of his message and mission." But at least Buddhist and Christian pluralists could agree that there is no problem with the continued existence of the two religions with two different conceptualizations of the ultimate.

The final Buddhist anthropomorphic figures that I will discuss are not well understood by many, but in my opinion they provide the most authentic way of incorporating Jesus into a Buddhist conceptual system. Therefore, these figures could be most productively contemplated by Christians interested in using Buddhist materials to expand their understandings of the Jesus of Christianity. The *yidams* of Vajrayana Buddhism, colorful beings who are depicted with great variety in Tibetan art, are anthropomorphic personifications of enlightened activity. These beings are of both genders, often with multiple heads and arms, portrayed in vivid primary colors, sometimes alone and sometimes in sexual embrace, sometimes wrathful and sometimes peaceful. Though outsiders are most familiar with them as art objects, their true significance is their esoteric use in meditation, as so-called meditation deities. They are visualized by the meditator, who also recites a liturgy explaining all the symbolism contained in the colors, attributes, and poses of these deities, performs hand gestures that express these meanings, and intones a mantra specific to the deity. There are many *yidams* in Vajrayana Buddhism and they are not ranked in a hierarchy. In a vague way, a certain *yidam* might be especially appropriate for a specific individual, stage of life, or situation, but this is a matter of utility, of method, of using the right tool for the job, not of right or wrong, correct or incorrect, conceptually.

These deities, however, are quite different from the deities of monotheistic religions, at least as their deities are usually understood by monotheists. As anthropomorphic representation of enlightenment, they are not metaphysically separate creators and saviors. As such, they are not ultimately separate from the meditator, who identifies with the deity by visualizing him or herself as the deity, using this method to wake up more quickly one's own enlightened qualities. In this kind of meditation, it is possible to relate fully with a deity emotionally without falling into the conceptual trap (from the Buddhist point of view) of metaphysical dualism.

To see Jesus as a *yidam* would probably seem incongruent to many Christians. Yet to me this is the most attractive and reasonable possibility of all. This may in some part be due to the fact that I myself, despite my personal history and my conceptual disagreement with much Christian conceptual apparatus, can appreciate Christian liturgy very deeply if I take it as Christian *sadhana,* thinking of it in much the same way that I think of Buddhist *sadhana* liturgies invoking the meditation deities with whom I have worked in my own practices. I must confess to occasional fantasy of what a *sadhana* invoking Jesus in *yab-yum* form would entail and how beneficial it could be!

There are also substantive reasons for suggesting this possibility. Using the criterion of utility, of assessing a religious phenomenon in terms of its effect on those who adhere to it, Jesus as the *yidam* of a Christian *sadhana* would encourage profound emotional, psychological, and spiritual transformation in those who performed this *sadhana.* This transformation, after all, is the important factor. My studies as a historian of religions lead me to suspect that all successful religious activity in fact does what is explicitly and consciously sought in the practice of *sadhana*—self-transformation, temporary and permanent, through using all human faculties (body, speech, and mind) in meditative or contemplative ritual. To do so through visualization of and identification with a *yidam* as anthropomorphic representation of enlightenment, as well as of one's own potential, is simply to be very explicit and self-aware about one's goals.

Interpreting Jesus as a *yidam* intersects in interesting ways with central Christian interpretations of Jesus as "the incarnate son of God." If we interpret Jesus as an incarnate son of God, with an emphasis on the incarnate *person* rather than on his *task* of atonement and redemption, the conversation can go in a direction quite different from usual Christian claims. Is it necessary to see Jesus as *uniquely* incarnate? The usual answer is yes. It is a truism that, while Christians are urged to be Christlike, no one of them aspires to become Christ. To me, as a Buddhist, this idea seems almost self-defeating. To put it most bluntly, to me it would be supremely frustrating to be told on the one hand that I should be Christlike, but on the other that I am condemned and predestined to failure in that central task. To see Jesus as model of incarnation rather than as sole possible example of incarnation would be so much more inspiring and attractive.[11] And that would be the effect of regarding Jesus as a *yidam* whose *sadhana* one practiced both in formal meditation and in life. Such an interpretation of Jesus would also mesh well with the most basic effect of incarnational theology, which is the sense of sacramental or sacred presence in the world that flows out of a theology of deity incarnate in the phenomenal world. A sense of sacred presence within the phenomenal world overcomes the remoteness of a transcendent deity and also overcomes the metaphysical dualism between deity and humanity.

Christians, however—even pluralist Christians—might well find my suggestion ludicrous and state cogent reasons why. I have anticipated at least some of their objections and could reply. First, they might say, the identification with Jesus is unacceptable and blasphemous. But I would suggest that if one is serious about the imitation of Christ, such meditations are rather effective means to that end. Second, many would say that *yidams* are clearly mythic projections, whereas Jesus is a historical character. My reply would be that the Jesus of Christianity, theologized as the second person of a trinity, is also highly mythic and that the Jesus of empirical history is untraceable. Religion is not made of empirical history; it is made of mythical history, of highly selective symbolic interpretations of historical events, even for those religions that are "historical." Jesus is effective and transformative for Christian piety of all levels of sophistication insofar as he functions as what Jungians would call an archetype, not because of his historical existence. I do not think such a statement psychologizes religion but rather explains how religious doctrines, which are mythic projections, work to transform their adherents.

However, I also have different reservations about the suggestions I have just made. They explain how I as a Buddhist would understand Jesus if I for some reason were compelled to fit Jesus into my religious universe. There is no real reason why I should do that, since I reject the Christian pluralists' claim for "the universality and indispensability of his message and mission." Nor do I presume that Christians should be attracted to my solution of what is essentially their problem—the meaning of the Jesus of Christianity to Christians who coinhabit a global village with non-Christians. I prefer, in the long run, to let the two myth and symbol systems stand as they are—unique, radically different, and magnificent. That solution, however, requires everyone to renounce exclusive and absolute claims for and about their conceptualizations of the ultimate. That includes Christians and their claims for the uniqueness, unsurpassability, finality, indispensability, and universality of Jesus! Except for that claim, he seems fine as he is and doesn't really need to be reconceptualized in Buddhist terms. I have never understood why Christians feel they would lose so much if they gave up those claims about Jesus. To me it seems they lose nothing important and would gain cohumanity with the rest of us.

NOTES

1. This essay was first prepared for a conference on Views of Jesus from the Perspectives of the World's Religions, held at Vivekananda Monastery and Retreat Center, Ganges, Michigan, September 1990. It has been substantially revised for publication.

2. Paul Griffiths, *Christianity through Non-Christian Eyes* (Maryknoll, New York: Orbis Books, 1990).

3. From the brochure announcing the conference for which this paper was initially written.

4. Paul Knitter, "Key Questions for a Theology of Religions," *Horizons* 17, no. 1 (1990), pp. 92–97.

5. Ibid., p. 97.

6. Griffiths, *Christianity through Non-Christian Eyes,* p. 236.

7. In Mahayana Buddhism, *upaya* and *prajna* are the two most important disciplines of and skills sought by a bodhisattva. Though both are equally important and necessary, and the goal of religious practice could be said to the "union of *upaya* and *prajna*," this union of the right and left hands brought in *anjali,* the mudra of folded hands, or the union of male and female in the sexual embrace of the *yab-yum* icon. In other words, this union is the union of nonduality, not the union of monism. This extremely subtle point cannot be overemphasized.

8. Ruhula Walpola, *What the Buddha Taught,* (New York: Grove Press, 1974), p. 11.

9. This is one of the most familiar metaphors for the multiplicity of *upaya.*

10. Griffiths, *Christianity through Non-Christian Eyes,* p. 164.

11. Interestingly, many Christian feminists are also suggesting that Jesus be seen as model of incarnation, rather than as sole representative of incarnation.

Christ as the Truth, the Light, the Life, but a Way?

BOKIN KIM

Won Buddhist Temple of Philadelphia

A CONSERVATIVE KOREAN Presbyterian pastor asks me what I know about Christ. He asks again what a Buddhist can know about Christ. He claims that Christ cannot be understood from other aspects of view, but only from the Christian view. Then what do I know at all about Christ?

My Buddhist understanding of Christ does not start with how Christ has been understood in the Christian context. My understanding is based on the reading of the Christian scripture. My reading of the scripture is guided by Sot'aesan's understanding of Christianity.[1]

According to my reading, the Bible presents two meanings of Christ: Christ in the transhistorical sense and Christ in the historical sense. The meaning of Christ as the Truth, the Light, and the Life represents a Christ in the transhistorical sense. The meaning of Christ as a way represents a Christ in the historical sense. Because Jesus did not make any distinction or clarification between these two meanings, it is obvious that even the Christian tradition has confusion on the meaning of Christ. As a result, most Christians hold to an exclusive view of Christ that claims his uniqueness.

My attribution of two meanings of Christ is derived from a similar distinction in Buddhism. Buddha in the transhistorical sense represents the universal nature of Buddha, which is identical with Truth. *Truth* can be replaced by other terms, such as *Light* or *Life*. Buddha in the historical sense means the historical nature of Buddha. In this sense, Buddha is unique and should not be depicted as absolute nor as universal. Likewise, Christ can be construed in these two ways.

CHRIST AS THE TRUTH, LIGHT, AND LIFE

When I read the description of Christ as the Truth, Light, and Life in the Gospel according to John, I feel a strong urge to replace *Christ* with the term *Buddha*—not Gautama Buddha but Dharmakaya Buddha. Here *Christ* refers to the source of the historical Christ just as Dharmakaya Buddha is the source of historical Buddha. In this sense, Christ cannot be compared with any beings in the world and thus is being described absolutely. Christ only is the Truth, Light, and Life. Similarly, there is a Zen koan saying, "Buddha alone exists."

Here the terms *Christ* and *Buddha* do not point to historical figures such as Jesus of Nazareth and Siddhartha Gautama. According to a story related to the compilation of Buddha's teaching, Ananda, who heard Buddha talk the most, was excluded from the committee of compilation. The reason was that Ananda saw the corporal aspect of the Buddha only, but he could not meet the spiritual aspect of the Buddha. The term *awakening* in the Buddhist tradition refers to understanding the absolute or universal nature within each transient being.

It seems wrong if one claims that only Christ, not Buddha, is the Truth, Light, or Life. By the same token it is wrong to say that Buddha alone, not Christ, exists in eternity. It is wrong to identify historical figures such as Jesus or Gautama with the Truth, Light, or Life. It is more erroneous to exclusively describe only one historical figure as the Truth, Light, or Life. According to my understanding, the terms *Christ* and *Buddha* are not the starting point for arguing the uniqueness of the historical Jesus or Gautama but for awakening our absolute or universal nature. That is, Christ as Truth, Light, and Life is our true nature or true self. In this nature there is no distinction between Christ and Buddha, between Christ and me, or between Buddha and me.

Regardless of how our foundation is named—Christ (or God), Buddha (Dharmakaya Buddha), Tao, or Wu-chi—our foundation is the basis from which religions are originated.

CHRIST AS A WAY

CHRIST IS A way to our foundation—in other words, the Truth, Light, and Life. Christ's way is faith/grace. Jesus taught that the faith in God and grace from God would bring forth salvation to the believers. Similarly, Buddha is a way to the Truth, Light, and Life. Buddha's way is practice/enlightenment, which is different from Christ's way. Buddha taught that one would achieve liberation through practice/ enlightenment. Christ's way—equal to Buddha's way—functions as a means to achieve the religious goal, whether salvation or liberation. Thus, Christ's way or Buddha's way is a way, not "The Way."

Now I will introduce Sot'aesan's description of Christ's way. Sot'aesan defined Christ's way as faith. Based on his encounters with Christian scriptures and members of Christian denominations, Sot'aesan characterizes the Christian faith as a "reliance on other power" and as having "no immediate contact with the source of faith, namely God without spirit being open."

One Encounter

The Great Master [Sot'aesan], as he returned from a sightseeing trip to Mt. Diamond said, "The innkeeper where I stayed at Mt. Diamond happened to be a Christian. He was so devout and enjoyed his life so much that I could not but ask him about his personal history. He told me that he had believed in God for thirty years, and that despite many obstacles he remained thankful. During good times he thanked God for being good to him, and during bad times he thanked God for correcting and guiding him. Thus, strengthened by his faith on every favorable or unfavorable occasion, he lived a happy life. . . . The Christian man was able to acquire a happy life even though he relied solely on his faith in the Power of Another's Ability without perceiving the source of Truth." (*The Scripture of Won Buddhism,* Faith 12)

Here the faith of the innkeeper—depicted as thankful for God on every occasion—is described as reliance on other power by Sot'aesan. Why is the innkeeper always thankful for God even during bad times? To him good times and bad times are not occurring incidentally, but they are given by God's love. An unfavorable occasion as well as favorable occasion is the mark of God's love. The unfavorable occasion occurs out of God's love as a way of showing an individual his wrongdoings. That is, God's love is given in order to set him on his guard against wrongdoings.

Sot'aesan describes the characteristics of the innkeeper's faith as "without perceiving the source of Truth." The innkeeper has not realized yet why God or God's love responds to him differently. The innkeeper partially perceives that the source of his faith is related to doing. He does not, however, have a clear understanding about the source of his faith; that is, he does not know whether the self or self-power is the source of faith.

According to Sot'aesan, complete faith is the integration of faith as other-reliance and faith as self-reliance. Thus, Sot'aesan suggests this integrated faith to the Christian tradition.

Another Encounter

When Cho, Song-Kwang came to see him for the first time, the Great Master said, "You look different from other people. What is your religion?" Song-Kwang answered, "I have been an elder in the Presbyterian Church for some years." The Great Master asked, "As you have believed in God for so many years, can you tell me where God is?" Song-Kwang replied, "God is omniscient and omnipresent. It is said that we see God everywhere." The Great Master asked again, "Then, have you seen him often, and have you heard him talk, and has God taught you directly?" Song-Kwang answered, "I have not seen him nor have I talked with him yet." The Great Master said, "Then you are still not qualified to be a true disciple of Jesus and have communion with him." Song-Kwang asked, "Pray tell me how to see God and how to be taught by God." The Great Master said, "If you constantly study so that you may become a true disciple of Jesus, you will see God and can be taught by God. . . . Even a Christian, if he deserves to be a true disciple of Jesus, will understand what I am doing. Also, my disciples who deserve to be my true disciples will understand what Jesus was doing." (*The Scripture of Won Buddhism,* Prospects for the Future 14)

Here Cho, Song-Kwang, an elder in the Presbyterian Church, is described as "having no immediate contact with God." The Presbyterian elder Cho has indirect contact with God through Jesus and only believes the message that Jesus spoke.

The elder Cho's faith, namely faith without immediate contact with God, shows that he has not become a true disciple of Jesus. The Gospel reads, "If you really knew me, you would know my father as well. From now on, you do know him and have seen him" (John 14:7). If one were a true disciple of Christ, one would know God, Sot'aesan emphasized. If one does not have contact with God, then one has not become a true disciple of Christ.

Sot'aesan understands that if one practices well, then one's spirit will be open. That is, as the completion of faith for a true disciple of Jesus, Sot'aesan talks about practicing well and one's spirit being open. If one is practicing well and makes their spirit open, one sees or hears God. Thus one becomes a true disciple of Jesus. The Gospel also talks about the work of the Spirit. The Gospel says, "I will send him [the Spirit] to you . . . when he, the Spirit of truth, comes, he will guide you into all truth" (John 16:7–13).

According to Sot'aesan's understanding, Christ's way is a way to understand other ways. Christ's way as well as other ways help us to reach the foundation. Though the gospel has a passage saying, "I am the Way. . . . No one comes to the Father except through me," Sot'aesan understands that others from different ways really reach the Father. Only "through me" does not mean exclusion of other ways but total devotion to Christ's way.

GRACE FROM CHRIST'S WAY

I UNDERSTAND CHRIST as a way, not as "The Way." I understand that Christ played a significant role to humanity. Faith as assurance is to go beyond ego-boundary and to point to the Truth, Light, and Life. As Paul says in his Epistle, "I no longer live, but Christ lives in me . . . I live by faith in the Son of God" (Gal. 2:20). That is, by faith, the ego-boundary is gone and eternity is gained.

What Buddhists garner when they follow Buddha's path is the realization of the emptiness of beings and the empty nature of ego. As the Heart Sutra says, nothing can be attained, thus I have no obstruction, nor fear. Therefore, I finally achieve nirvana. That is, realization of nothingness or emptiness is the way to freedom and eternity.

A Christian's radical faith or a Buddhist's radical awakening serve the same goal—that is, how to go beyond ego-boundary. A Christian's faith is based on God's grace, where believers totally rely on God. The Spirit guides them to go beyond the limitation of self and achieve eternity. That is, Christians go beyond their ego-boundary while relying on other power. On the other hand, Buddhists can reach radical awakening by their strenuous effort of practice. Practice leads them to realize the true nature of self and to achieve freedom from the ego-boundary. That is, Buddhists rely on self power for radical awakening.

As a Buddhist I feel that Buddhist self-effort is not an easy way. Often self-effort leads us toward the opposite of the Truth. Though the Truth is formulated as the empty nature of self, self-effort or practice in Buddhism hardens the shell of self far away from the truth of emptiness. Arrogance or an inconsiderate attitude are often derived from the wrong view that is created from practice or self-effort.

Paul's faith seems a good example of radical faith in Christianity. Though he is challenged by his egoistic desire after his dramatic experience of conversion, his firm faith leads him to defeat his ego-boundary. Based on his experience, Paul strongly guides people to oneness with Christ. Christian faith, that is, faith in Christ as the savior, is truly a grace that leads one to go beyond one's ego-boundary.

As a Buddhist I understand that a Christian's faith in Christ—which helps the believer to go beyond one's ego-boundary—is equal to a Buddhist's faith in Dharmakaya Buddha or Truth. Based on faith in Christ, Christians attain salvation, or eternity. Similarly, Buddhists attain nirvana— namely freedom based on their faith in the Truth. In this context Buddhists also start with faith. Without faith a Buddhist practice for nirvana cannot be initiated. Though Buddhism does not emphasize that awakening is directly derived from faith, the Hwayen Sutra teaches that radical faith is equal to awakening.

Faith is a significant religious experience shared among Buddhists and Christians. Then why does Paul's conversion in Christianity or Hwayen's radical faith in Buddhism not occur to people easily? How can one have faith at all? There seem to be various views on these questions. Buddhists—whose explanations are very different from Christian ones— seem to start with what one can do now with one's self-power. Thus, Buddhists focus more on practice than faith because the occurrence of faith itself is very mysterious.

The tradition of Christianity, however, has placed more focus on faith. Christian believers follow the way of faith and live their lives with selfless giving, while going beyond the boundary of ego. As a Buddhist I feel the mysterious power within the Christian tradition, which has been trans- forming millions of people for centuries. I wonder, however, whether the faith of the Christian tradition is going to be an effective way or not in the future. If not, what kind of path does Christianity need to create?

NOTES

1. Sot'aesan, Chungbin Park (1891–1943) is the founder of Won Buddhism, a reformed Buddhism started in Korea eighty years ago. Sot'aesan had twenty years' journey of searching the Truth. After his Great Awakening he encountered scriptures and believers from different religious traditions. There are written several episodes of Sot'aesan's meeting with Christian believers in *The Scripture of Won Buddhism.*

BIBLIOGRAPHY

The Holy Bible: New International Version. 1984.
Pal Khn Chon (trans.). *The Scripture of Won Buddhism.* Iksan, Korea: Won Buddhism Pub- lishing, 1988.

Jesus, Man of Sin: Toward a New Christology in the Global Era

SOHO MACHIDA

Princeton University

SIN AS THE COMMON GROUND

THE BLASPHEMOUS TITLE of this article is likely to outrage more than a few devout Christians. I am aware that most Christians view Jesus as the most immaculate and beautiful person who ever lived. As a Buddhist scholar and practitioner, however, I cannot extinguish a long-held question from my mind. Was Jesus really free from sin? I do not object to the view of those Christians who see him as the greatest living expression of compassion and courage. But the Christian construction of an untainted, perfect image of Jesus, the Son of God, raises certain problems that I would like to address. Although Jesus, the Anointed, could have had a special mission in the human world, the Son of Man did not appear as the Holy Ghost. He was incarnated in human form: "And the Word became flesh and dwelt among us, full of grace and truth; we have beheld his glory, glory as of the only son from the Father" (John 1:14).

It is important to carefully consider the meaning of the Incarnation. The fact that Jesus came to be born with flesh in this world means that he chose to stand on the common ground of sin with us. The sin that I refer to here is the most ontologically fundamental sin that is at the core of human experience. What links us with Jesus is none other than so-called Original Sin.

To be sure, as a man who comes from a different religious tradition, I do not make this outrageous claim because I want to dispute the value of the divine personhood of Jesus, or because I am cynical about the most sacred object of Christian faith. I have a deep respect for the greatness of the Christian tradition that has developed around this very unusual person, Jesus Christ.

On a personal level too, I do not think of Jesus as a distant figure, as merely the god of another religion. During my boyhood in Japan, I often attended an Episcopal church; and the first academic degree I earned in the United States was in theological studies. In light of all that I have learned from my own personal involvement with Christianity, I still believe that Jesus was a person who suffered like us as a sinful human being.

If I were to choose the most important of Jesus' words from the Bible, I would not hesitate to point to the following passage: "*Eloi, Eloi, lema sabachthani?* (My God, my God, why have you deserted me?)" (Mark 15:34). It is surprising how few Christian scholars have offered persuasive interpretations of these words, which Jesus is said to have uttered in the final moments of his life. Many Christians would rather not hear such contradictory, despairing words come from the mouth of Jesus. Yet these words of extreme suffering contain the key message at the core of Christian faith.

Though I am also interested in Jesus' historical background and the political role he played in a tiny corner of the Roman Empire, it is not the purpose of this article to investigate the historicity of Jesus' life, as many theologians and historians have attempted to do in recent years. I will focus instead on the philosophical implications of Jesus' life and his physical body, and why I believe it is important to develop a new Christology for the coming global era.

THE KARMIC BODY OF JESUS

FIRST, WHY DID Jesus have to experience the suffering of crucifixion? The evident answer might be explained this way: because he sacrificed himself to redeem the human race, which has been sinning since the time of Adam and

Eve. I would like, however, to suggest a totally different answer: Jesus was crucified to atone for his own sin. He courageously showed the way each of us must take responsibility for our own lives. He deserves our high admiration, but not excessive mystification.

I do not mean that Jesus committed any specific sin in his lifetime, but rather that as the Son of Man he too was equally burdened with Original Sin, which is at the core of human existence. Anyone born into a human body cannot be free from Original Sin. Before we deify Jesus, we must first boldly examine his human nature: "And he began to teach them that the Son of Man must suffer many things. . . . And he said this plainly. And Peter took him, and began to rebuke him. But turning and seeing his disciples, he rebuked Peter, and said, Get behind me, Satan! For you are not on the side of God, but of men" (Mark 8:31–33). If Jesus were completely transcendent, he would not have had to "suffer many things." He suffered just like us, and that is why we feel close to him. Jesus' rebuke of Peter also indicates that he considered himself to be not God, but a man.

In an ontological sense, the Christian concept of Original Sin is roughly equivalent to the Buddhist notion of karma. Karma is "a link which connects an act and its fruition, lasting until the fruit becomes ripe."[1] In Buddhism, all beings are believed to carry their accumulated karma throughout endless cycles of transmigration spanning the past, present, and future. Karma created by past actions determines circumstances in this lifetime. In other words, the karma at the core of one's being determines the unfolding pattern of one's life and self-identity at any given moment.

One well-known Buddhist text, the *Milindapanha,* gives an account of a serious discussion that took place between the Greek king Milinda and a scholarly Buddhist priest called Nāgasena, about whether or not the Buddha himself is subject to the consequences of his own karma, as when he was injured by an enemy who attacked him: "For Devadatta, O King, had harbored hatred against the Tathāgata during a succession of hundreds of thousands of births. It was in his hatred that he seized hold of a mighty mass of rock, and pushed it over with the hope that it would fall upon his head. But two other rocks came together, and intercepted it before it had reached the Tathāgata; and by the force of their impact a splinter was torn off, and fell upon the Blessed One's foot, and made it bleed. Now this pain must have been produced in the Blessed One either as the result of his own Karma, or of some one else's act. For beyond these two there can be no other kind of pain."[2]

Devadatta's hatred of Śākyamuni was rooted in the fact that Śākyamuni, before he became a wandering mendicant and started his own religious community, had been married to a young woman, Yashodharā, with whom Devadatta was in love. The above discourse examines the important question of whether all beings, including the Awakened One, are subject to the effects of past karma. Nāgasena recognizes the difference between his own view and that of the Brahmans, who believe that even the Buddha was not exempt from the effects of the karma generated by his previous actions. Here Nāgasena refutes their argument: "So, O King, it is not all pain that is the result of Karma. And you should accept as a fact that when the Blessed One became a Buddha he had burnt out all evil from within him."[3] The Buddha's injury is explained simply as a physical phenomenon, without any connection to the notion of karma. However, the priest's last statement suggests the view that Śākyamuni also had evil in himself before he "burnt" it away when he attained nirvana. There is no assumption that the Buddha was pure and immaculate from the moment of birth. In other words, evil was an important element in the transformation of a human being called Śākyamuni into the Blessed One, the Buddha.

The Yogācāra school of Buddhism describes the mechanism of consciousness in which karma is produced: "Existence (*samsāra*) is explained in terms of the "store consciousness." The evolution or transformation of this "store consciousness" is without beginning (*anādikālika*). The cyclic evolution takes place in the following manner: As the seeds of karma mature in the "store consciousness," the second transformation, or the evolution of *manas,* takes place. Then comes the third transformation—the evolution of the perceptive consciousness (*pravrtti-vijnāna),* consisting of subject-object discrimination. This perceptive consciousness leads to activity or behavior (*karma),* good, bad, or indeterminate."[4] All our memories of the past have accumulated in the *ālayav-ijnāna.* As these memories mature, they erupt and are manifested in this life (*samsāra*) as various forms of suffering. The pervasive qualities of ignorance and desire are essentially "resultant (*vipāka*) because it represents the germination of the seeds (*bīja*), which are the dispositions (*vāsanā*) of good and bad actions and which have attained maturity (*paripāka*)."[5]

This very source of suffering, however, is also the locale of the blossom of our spiritual liberation, because it is only through our "karma-body" (*karma-vipāka*) that the dharma, or ultimate truth, manifests itself. As suggested by the Buddhist metaphor of the white lotus blooming in the midst of a muddy swamp, the body of sinfulness becomes the locus for spiritual awakening. Without our karma-body, the dharma would lose its topos of manifestation. In the same vein, the Incarnation means that Jesus received the body of Original Sin for the sole purpose of exercising God's will in this world; no suffering, no nirvana; no sin, no Resurrection.

Therefore, it is not quite logical for Christians to claim that Jesus was immaculate from birth. I believe that it is essential to recognize Jesus' body of karma, or sinfulness. I am not sure why Christians hasten to deny the corporeality of Jesus. To praise his divinity, we first need his physical body as the topos where the Divine intersects with the Human. The weakness of Christian teaching lies in its neglect of corporeality as an essential element of religious experience.

Furthermore, we must recognize the evil element of the incarnated Jesus. Christians have a lot to say about the Holy Spirit (pneuma), but very little to say about the evil spirit (legion). Yet where there is light, there is shadow, and vice versa. Jesus himself suggests that our lives are shadowed by our own evil thoughts: "What comes from your heart is what makes you unclean. Out of your heart come evil thoughts, vulgar deeds, stealing, murder, unfaithfulness in marriage, greed, meanness, deceit, indecency, envy, insults, pride, and foolishness. All of these come from your heart, and they are what make you unfit to worship God" (Mark 7:20–23).

The mind is like a haunted house that we have not yet completely explored. The underworld of human nature is unfathomably deep. Jesus shared this darkness with us. Let me quote one of my favorite parables in the Bible: "The scribes and the Pharisees brought a woman who had been caught in adultery, and placing her in the midst. . . . Jesus bent down and wrote with his finger on the ground. And as they continued to ask him, he stood up and said to them, 'Let him who is without sin among you be the first to throw a stone at her.' And once more he bent down and wrote with his finger on the ground" (John 8:3–8).

It is strange that no explanation is given about what Jesus was writing with his finger on the ground. In that silent gesture, was he not perhaps revealing an awareness within himself of the same evil nature as the woman's? For one who shares in the common awareness of sin, it is impossible to judge another. Jesus' attitude of love and tolerance toward weak and sinful ordinary people may originate not necessarily in his sacredness, but rather in his bond of sympathy with all other human beings as a Man of Sin.

I would not be surprised to learn that earnest members of the Christian community are already upset with my unconventional claim; but there are also Christians who would agree with me. The so-called Hidden Christians who lived about two hundred years ago in Japan are one example. They remained faithful to Christian teachings even throughout a period of intense persecution by the Tokugawa regime. In *The Beginning of the Heaven and Earth* (*Tenchi hajimarino koto*), the sacred text these Japanese Christians secretly transmitted for generations, there is an astonishing description of Jesus' prayer at Gethsemane: "In this forest the Holy One received an oracle from Deus: 'Thousands of infants lost their lives on your account. I fear they may now forfeit the pleasure of Paraiso. For their sake in the next world, you must be tortured and trodden upon, suffer and give up your body.' The Holy One then fell suddenly to the ground, and beads of sweat and blood poured down from him."[6]

This refers to the story of King Herod having murdered thousands of newborn infants when he was searching for Jesus. Because in that sense Jesus has deprived the infants' souls of the opportunity to enter Paraiso (Paradise), he is ordered by Deus (God) to "suffer and give up your body" to atone for his own sin.

We must take care not to judge the faith of the Hidden Christians too hastily as a mere distortion or misunderstanding of the original Christian teachings, because it is the genuine faith for which they risked their lives in the face of torture and persecution. The Hidden Christians' concepts of evil, sin, and forgiveness contain many interesting elements that merit thoughtful examination. Their unique position within Christian tradition sometimes makes me wonder if their less dichotomous, more inclusive faith might suggest a future direction of religious evolution for both Christianity and Buddhism.

Jesus on the Cross

Jesus always remained sympathetic with people on the fringes of human society, such as tax collectors and prostitutes. In order to truly forgive and accept these people, he had to embrace them completely, which meant embracing their sinfulness. He transmitted God's transcendent message by touching people with loving hands. Jesus' greatness lay not in his power as a worker of miracles but in the courage and compassion he demonstrated in closing the gap between himself and those around him.

Crucifixion was the inevitable consequence of his choice to share in the pain and suffering of humanity. Even so, at first he hesitated to choose that path. In the voice of Jesus at Gethsemane, we sense the painful inner struggle he must have gone through: "And he took with him Peter and James and John, and began to be greatly distressed and troubled. And he said to them, 'My soul is very sorrowful, even to death; remain here, and watch.' And going a little farther, he fell on the ground and prayed that, if it were possible, the hour might pass from him. And he said, 'Abba, Father, all things are possible to thee; remove this cup from me; yet not what I will, but what thou wilt'" (Mark 14:33–36). Jesus' agony reminds me of the Buddha's long and difficult path to nirvana. The Buddha risked his life by undergoing extremely ascetic spiritual practices and struggled against demons as he sat in meditation beneath the bo tree, the spot where he eventually attained enlightenment.

On the day of the Crucifixion, Jesus, wearing torn clothes and a crown of thorns on his head, walks to Golgotha in a state of great distress. The scene dramatically symbolizes the hardships that anyone is likely to experience in the process of psychological growth. Jesus refuses to drink the wine mixed with a drug to ease his pain; he is fully prepared to accept, without compromise, the sin he shares with humankind. And finally he mumbles these words of despair on the Cross: "*Eloi, Eloi, lema sabachthani?* (My God, my God, why have you deserted me?)" (Mark 15:34). We should never attempt to rationally interpret these words merely in order to glorify Jesus. Otherwise, the gem of Christian faith may be lost. This is the ultimate expression of anguish that came out of Jesus' mouth when he touched the darkness of sin (karma) that is at the core of human existence. The Passion was utterly tragic—but the extreme of despair is the beginning of hope. From a Christian perspective, the moment of Jesus' death became the moment of the birth of God's great work on earth.

In *The Logic of the Place of Nothingness and the Religious Worldview,* Nishida Kitarō suggests that a human being encounters the Absolute only through complete self-negation: "The religious standpoint must negate character absolutely. This absolute negation does not mean mere death, which is death in relative opposition to life—death as the affair of merely human reality, which must be negated absolutely. We must die to human life and death; therein lies absolute life. Thus absolute death is absolute life, and absolute negation is absolute affirmation. But to attain such absolute negation we must transcend the spirit and culture, to deepen the awareness of self-contradiction and sin concealed at the bottom of free will."[7]

The Crucifixion is the moment Jesus fully accepted "the self-contradiction and sin concealed at the bottom of free will." In reality, Jesus was rejected by both Romans and Jews, and he failed to survive in human society. Only through this failure could Jesus' earthly ego be completely destroyed and God's presence finally manifested on earth. Nishida writes about this paradox: "Death involves a relative being facing an absolute. For the self to face God is to die. When Isaiah saw God he cried out: 'Woe to me! For I am undone; because I am a man of unclean lips; for my eyes have seen the King, the Lord of hosts' [Isaiah 6:5]. What is relative cannot be said to stand up against an absolute. Conversely, an absolute that merely opposes the relative is not the true absolute; for in that case, it would merely be relative, too. When a relative being faces the true absolute it cannot exist. It must pass over into nothing. The living self itself relates to the divine, encounters the divine, only through dying—only in this paradoxical form."[8]

We know that the Holy Spirit entered the body of Jesus at the baptism of John, but in Jesus there was still an undeniable gap between flesh and spirit. His extreme language and behavior, which can be observed here and there in the Bible, may be attributed to this gap. Jesus finally found the solution to this dichotomy on the Cross, the topos where spirit and flesh, light and darkness, divine and human, good and evil, intersect. At that moment, Jesus' body of karma accomplished its goal of transforming the Man of Sin into the Son of

God, the Savior. Only on the Cross, Jesus finally became "truly Man, and truly God" as defined in the Councils of Nicaea (325) and Chalcedon (451). "Yet a little while, and the world will see me no more, but you will see me; because I live, you will live also. In that day you will know that I am in my Father, and you in me, and I in you" (John 14:19–20).

The myth of Christ's resurrection three days after the crucifixion symbolizes the birth of a new consciousness in humankind. This new consciousness transcends the dichotomous boundary between the infinite and the finite, the sacred and the profane, and ultimately unites Jesus Christ and ourselves.

AFFIRMING EVIL

IF WE UNDERSTAND the meaning of the sin that was intrinsic to Jesus' human form, we must reconsider his relationship with Judas. To view the two of them as the Son of God and his traitor is an overly simplistic and superficial interpretation. It was indeed Judas Iscariot who betrayed Jesus for thirty silver coins, but his cruel act of betrayal concretely embodies the evil inherent in every human being. When we truly see the evil within ourselves, we realize that Judas is none other than "me" and "you." I would even go so far as to suggest that Judas reflects another aspect of Jesus.

Negating the evil within Jesus and ourselves does not glorify anyone or anything. On the contrary, if we hope the world's religions will one day find a common ground of universal understanding, we must first recognize the existence of evil as an essential element in humanity.

The Japanese Pure Land Buddhist priest Shinran (1173–1262) emphasized the salvific power of Amida Buddha, which enabled him to accept even that evil that was "like snakes and scorpions" within himself. The first section of his great work, the *Tannishō,* clearly reveals his feeling toward Amida, the Absolute: "At the very moment the desire to call the Nembutsu is awakened in us in the firm faith that we can attain rebirth in the Pure Land through the saving grace of the Inconceivable Grand Vow, the all-embracing, none-forsaking virtue of Amida is conferred on us. Know that in Amida's Grand Vow there is no distinction of young and old, good and evil, that the Faith-Mind alone is essential, for it is the Vow to save all sentient beings, who are heavily burdened with sin and consumed with tormenting cravings. Once belief in Amida's Vow is established, no other virtue is necessary, for there is no goodness that surpasses Nembutsu. Evils are not feared, because no evil can hinder the fulfilling of Amida's Grand Vow."[9]

Shinran was keenly aware of his own sinfulness, and because of this he ultimately discovered the light of Amida's unconditional salvation. Amida has not atoned for Shinran's sin; instead, Amida accepts Shinran's whole being.

More important is the fact that we share the evil not only with other human beings, but with God himself. As Rudolf Otto attests in *The Idea of the Holy*, religious experience is always accompanied by an overwhelming sense of the holy, the numinous: "Religious dread would perhaps be a better designation. Its antecedent state is 'daemonic dread' with its queer perversion, a sort of abortive offshoot, the 'dread of ghosts.' It first begins to stir in the feeling of 'something uncanny,' 'eerie,' or 'weird.' It is this feeling which, emerging in the mind of primeval man, forms the starting point for the entire religious development in history."[10]

The demonic aspect of the holy arouses a feeling of "awfulness" (*tremendum*) which is not very far from "the mind of primeval man." It would be one-sided to focus only on the positive side of the divine in the form of light, love, generosity, and forgiveness. There is a dark side to God's sacredness, which is typically observed in Yahweh, a wrathful and jealous God. Jesus, who is, after all, directly descended from the lineage of Yahweh, exhibits traces of his fierce personality, as we can observe in a few scenes in the Bible: "And Jesus entered the temple of God and drove out all who sold and bought in the temple, and he overturned the tables of the money-changers and the seats of those who sold pigeons" (Matt. 21:12–13).

This was a familiar scene at that time in the temple of Jerusalem. Jesus may have acted in the name of righteousness; but from the standpoint of common sense, his violent act does not sound like that of a sacred being. In the eyes of the merchants and shoppers whom Jesus interrupted, he must have appeared more like a demon. His hostile actions continue: "In the morning, as he was returning to the city, he was hungry. And seeing a fig tree by the wayside he went to it, and found nothing on it but leaves only. And he said to it, 'May no fruit ever come from you again!' And the fig tree withered at once" (Matt. 21:19–20).

Here Jesus curses an innocent plant. Despite his principle teaching, "Love your neighbor," he is extremely hostile toward those who do not follow his teaching. If he were totally free from evil nature, he could not harbor a feeling of such hostility toward anyone or anything. His actions imply that evil is an essential aspect of the divine. In *Psychology and Religion,* C. G. Jung refers to this problem in terms of the Christian symbolism of the Trinity: "I cannot omit calling attention to the interesting fact that whereas the central Christian symbolism is a Trinity, the formula of the unconscious mind is a quaternity. As a matter of fact, even the orthodox Christian formula is not quite complete, because the dogmatic aspect of the evil principle is absent from the Trinity, the former leading a more or less awkward existence as devil."[11]

As Jung aptly points out, Christianity has not properly dealt with the problem of evil. Evil is always treated as something unwelcome and unwanted: "Over the hillside a large herd of pigs was feeding. So the evil spirits begged Jesus, 'Send us into those pigs! Let us go into them.' Jesus let them go, and they went out of the man and into the pigs. The whole herd of about two thousand pigs rushed down the steep bank into the lake and drowned" (Mark 5:11–13). This parable clearly illustrates the Christian view that evil spirits are external to oneself, rather than an element of human nature. This view sharply contrasts with the Buddhist idea that the evil in the world is a reflection of our own thoughts, impulses, and emotions.

The misinterpretation of evil has given rise to serious conflicts throughout Christian history. The dichotomy of good and evil, self and other that constitutes the essence of Christian teaching has been manifested in a long history of confrontations and persecutions around the world. Early Christians knew to some extent how to deal with evil through mythology and ritual, probably through the influence of indigenous European folk beliefs; but in modern times Christians tend to exclude evil from the sacred pantheon. This is actually a dangerous tendency, because neglecting evil invites its retaliation. Along these same lines, we should ask ourselves why our modern democratic society continues to give rise to an endless resurgence of radical groups such as the Ku Klux Klan and right-wing militant organizations.

In a larger context, we may be able to say that the ethical and political principles of Western civilization are deeply rooted in the Christian dichotomy of good versus evil. This civilization of confrontation, structured according to the framework of the Immaculate Jesus and Traitor Judas, can be found at every turn of our litigation-infested contemporary society.

Although on the surface it appears that Americans are becoming more and more indifferent to Christianity, the basic structure of the American mentality is still heavily influenced by Christian tradition, particularly the Puritan spirit. Americans can be fair minded and ambitious, but they can also be judgmental and discriminate harshly against those who do not share their values. How do we explain the intense hostility between advocates of pro-life and pro-choice positions on abortion, for example? What about prejudice against members of a particular race or against homosexuals? At a basic level this society illustrates the stark contrast between the haves and the have-nots, not only materially but in every aspect of human life. One stands as the Victor and the other bends as the Loser. It is like a déjà vu reflection of the immaculate Jesus and traitor Judas.

My advocacy for a new Christology is motivated not only by an impulse toward greater theological development, but also for the sake of achieving a better understanding of human life. I expect that Christianity will play a vital role in constructing a more tolerant and inclusive society for the millenium.

CHRISTIAN FAITH RECONSIDERED

I WOULD LIKE to call Christians' attention to three practical issues in particular. Christianity is one of the most influential religions in the modern world. If Christians were to adjust their attitudes even slightly in order to meet the growing spiritual needs of humankind, the global community would become a place of mutual respect and harmony.

First, there is the question of charity, the Christian attitude toward less fortunate members of society. Christianity has a glorious history of philanthropy. No other religion has ever produced figures like Albert Schweitzer or Mother Teresa, whose lives have become monuments to humankind's goodwill.

Christianity has contributed immeasurably to a wider recognition of human rights around the world. There are also many impressive stories about patients with fatal diseases or prison inmates who recover their hope for life through converting to Christianity. And while most Asian religions educate believers to passively resign themselves to their fates, Christianity is much more dynamic in transforming the world, encouraging people to act courageously in the face of adversity and to become model citizens. Christians show their commitment by becoming God's tools for constructing the Kingdom of Heaven in this world. When their sacrificial acts are carried out in the name of God, there is no room left for egotism. That is why their selfless actions are universally admired.

But Christians must exercise caution here as well. They must carry out their sacrificial acts with the awareness that they are no different from all other sinful beings. If they have the slightest consciousness of themselves as the superior helping the inferior or the faithful saving the unfaithful, they immediately lose their Christian dignity. Some Christian activists, contrary to their own ethical motivations, retain an unnecessarily strong self-consciousness or even hostility toward the rest of society.

Second, I propose that Christians reexamine the implications of what being a Christian means. To be a Christian should not merely depend on whether or not one has been baptized. Going to church, listening to sermons, and reading the Bible do not guarantee that one is a devout Christian.

I believe that the path of Christian faith should be defined by a much more stringent set of criteria. Christians cannot be exempted from self-reflection simply by believing that Jesus Christ atoned for their sins through the Passion. To believe that Jesus takes all the burdens from one's shoulders is to evade one's responsibility as a human being. Jesus demanded great sacrifice from those who wished to follow him: "And he called to him the multitude with his disciples, and said to them, 'If any man would come after me, let him deny himself and take up his cross and follow me. For whoever would save his life will lose it; and whoever loses his life for my sake and the gospel's will save it'" (Mark 8:34–35). Jesus does not say that he will carry the cross for us. What is implied here is that he will walk with us, sharing our sweat and toil on the way to the Kingdom of Heaven. Some Christians are not ready to go to all this trouble, and pretend instead to stay in the safety zone of lofty self-righteousness. Worst of all, they may even look down on those who do not have Christian faith. History tells us that many Christian missionaries exhibited this kind of arrogance when they traveled to different parts of the globe in past centuries.

If Christians are really determined to sacrifice themselves, to be crucified along with their own burden of sin, they must find in themselves a greater sympathy with people of all religions—even atheists. We all must become much more sensitive to the religious, cultural, ethnic, and ideological diversity in our global community. There is no one truth, and there is no one superior religion. This simple fact must be humbly accepted by many Christians who think otherwise.

To enter into the world of Christian faith means to walk with Jesus the long path to Golgotha. We may be humiliated, beaten, burdened with the heavy cross we carry on our shoulders. If each of us truly realized that we too could be nailed to the cross by our hands and legs, we would tremble before the grave implications of having faith in Christ. I personally know some Christians who abandoned their faith when they went through unbearably bitter experiences. I feel great sympathy with them—but at the same time, I believe that if Christianity were equipped with a more precise view of evil, they would not have had to go so far as to apostatize. In this respect, Buddhism is much more systematic in teaching us about how to view the incomprehensible and mysterious aspects of life.

Finally, I would like to offer a related opinion about Christian iconography. In Asia, Christianity has not spread as much as it has in other regions of the world. This is largely due to severe restrictions imposed by political systems in Asia; but it also has to do with the bloody image of Christ on the Cross. We must possess very strong nerves to accept as the object of daily worship the image of the bloody, starving Christ, with torn clothes and an unshaven beard. The image is neither soothing nor aesthetic. By contrast, images of the Buddha in nirvana make anyone who looks at them feel a sense of peace and contentment. Joy is one of the most important elements in Christian teaching, yet it is not sufficiently expressed through Christian icons. "I tell you for certain that you will cry and be sad, but the world will be happy. You will be sad, but later you will be happy. When a woman is about to give birth, she is in great pain. But after it is all over, she forgets the pain and is happy, because she has brought a child into the world. You are now very sad. But later I will see you, and you will be so happy that no one will be able to change the way they feel" (John 16:20–22).

If Jesus feels this joy within himself, artistic representations of his face should reveal it more explicitly. I would like to see the image of a smiling Jesus more often. Rather than focusing on Jesus suffering on the Cross, I wonder why Christian tradition does not pay more attention to the glorious figure of Christ who stood at the crossing of humanity and divinity by overcoming the eternal dichotomy of spirit and flesh, good and evil.

All religions continue to evolve. In this article I have focused on several problems in Christianity. Just as Christianity must change and progress, so too must Buddhism. I look forward to witnessing the mutually beneficial growth of these two religions in the future.

NOTES

1. Nakamura Hajime, *Indian Buddhism: A Survey with Bibliographical Notes* (Delhi: Motilal Banarsidass, 1987), p. 126.

2. F. Max Muller, ed., *The Sacred Books of the East* (Oxford: Claredon Press, 1890), vol. 35, p. 193.

3. Ibid., p. 195.

4. David J. Kalupahana, *Buddhist History: A Historical Analysis* (Honolulu: University of Hawai'i Press, 1976), p. 148.

5. Ibid., p. 147.

6. Christal Whelan, *The Beginning of Heaven and Earth: The Sacred Book of Japan's Hidden Christians* (Honolulu: University of Hawai'i Press, 1996), p. 57.

7. Takayama Tetsuo, *Nishida Tetsugaku* (Tokyo: Iwanami shoten, 1975), p. 292.

8. Nishida Kitaro, *Last Writings,* trans. David A. Dilworth (Honolulu: University of Hawai'i Press, 1960), p. 68.

9. *Tannishō: A Tract Deploring Heresies of Faith* (Kyoto: Higashi Honganji, 1961), p. 2.

10. Rudolf Otto, *The Idea of the Holy* (New York: Oxford University Press, 1958), p. 14.

11. C. G. Jung, *Psychology and Religion* (New Haven: Yale University Press, 1938), p. 73.

CHRISTIAN RESPONSES

Jesus and Buddhism:
A Christian View

Marcus J. Borg

Oregon State University

Like several of the contributors to this collection of essays, I begin with my own vantage point. By profession a historian of Jesus and Christian origins, I am by confession a Christian of a nonliteralist and nonexclusivist kind (once Lutheran, now Episcopalian). As a Christian, I am interested in the theological implications of my work as a historian. As a student of Buddhism, I am an amateur whose knowledge is limited to what I have learned from teaching world religions at the introductory undergraduate level.

The essays illustrate a classic issue in interreligious dialogue: What shall we compare? Exoteric forms or esoteric core? If Buddhism (esoteric or exoteric) is compared with external forms of popular-level Christianity over the centuries, the gulf is great indeed. But if we compare the historical Jesus and the mystical stream of Christianity (its internal core) with Buddhism, then there are important points of contact.

As a Jesus scholar and a Christian, I address two central subjects raised by the essays, the first more historical and the second more theological. I briefly compare the historical Jesus and the Buddha and then reflect about the exclusivist and absolutist claims made about Jesus by the most common forms of Christianity.

THE HISTORICAL JESUS AND THE BUDDHA

JESUS WAS A JEWISH mystic. This is radical shorthand for my fuller five-stroke sketch, as well as foundational for it. As a Jewish mystic (or Spirit person, by which I mean the same thing), Jesus became a healer, wisdom teacher, social prophet, and movement founder.[1] This sketch is the basis for comparing the historical Jesus and the Buddha.

Of the contributors, José Cabezón says the most about recent historical Jesus scholarship. I agree with him about much. Both Jesus and the Buddha opened up the religious life to marginalized people, stressed the interior life, and inaugurated reformist movements. Both traditions take spirits and "magic" seriously.[2] I agree that the major difference is Jesus much greater emphasis on social justice, which leads to a further difference: Jesus was killed, his life cut short because he was a social prophet, whereas the Buddha died from food poisoning. Jesus' public activity was thus very brief, perhaps as little as a year, compared to the forty or fifty years of the Buddha.

To return to similarities, I cite two more. Both Jesus and the Buddha had transforming enlightenment experiences of a mystical kind at about age thirty. Both became teachers of a convention-subverting wisdom flowing out of their enlightenment experiences.

Because Cabezón expresses uncertainty about the second claim, I summarize the reasons why I see Jesus as a teacher of an enlightenment way of wisdom similar to that taught by the Buddha.[3] "Seeing" (enlightenment) is strongly emphasized not only in sayings of Jesus but also in the metaphorical "spin" given to some of the stories reporting the healing of blindness. Moreover, inviting a new way of seeing is the primary rhetorical function of Jesus' aphorisms and parables, his most common forms of teaching.

Furthermore, imagery of "the way" is central to Jesus and the gospels, pointing to a foundational similarity to the teaching of the Buddha. There is the broad way and there is the narrow way; those who humble (empty) themselves will be exalted; the path to a new way of being involves dying to an old way of being. This emphasis points to an internal spiritual-psychological process very similar to Buddhist "emptying" and "letting go." "Dying" and "letting go" are metaphorical synonyms.[4]

Jesus' way undermined convention and affirmed a radical recentering in that which is beyond the domestications generated by convention: the sacred. As a mystic, Jesus knew this from his own experience.[5] Like the Buddha, he taught differently because he had seen differently.

Thus I have become persuaded of a foundational similarity between "the way" taught by the Buddha and "the way" taught by Jesus.[6] I tell my students that if Jesus and the Buddha were ever to meet, neither would try to convert the other—not because they would regard the task as hopeless, but because they would recognize each other.

I add one further comment about the historical Jesus. Namely, with the majority of today's Jesus scholars, I do not see the understanding of Jesus' death as a sacrifice for sin as going back to Jesus himself, but as one of several post-Easter metaphors interpreting the meaning of his death. The other metaphors include seeing Jesus' death as the defeat of the powers, as disclosure of God's love, and as embodiment of the way or path of transformation.

Moreover, in its first-century context, the sacrificial understanding of Jesus' death was a radically subversive metaphor. Temple theology claimed an institutional monopoly on access to God: some sins and impurities could be dealt with only through sacrifices offered in the temple. In this context, to say "Jesus is the sacrifice" negated this claim: the "once for all sacrifice" had been made. Thus "Jesus is the sacrifice" was initially a metaphorical proclamation of the immediacy of access to God apart from institutional mediation. As such, it affirmed that which was also at the heart of Jesus' own teaching: a way of transformation that subverted tradition.[7]

THE EXCLUSIVIST AND ABSOLUTIST CLAIMS OF CHRISTIANITY

ALL OF THE essayists cite problems generated by exclusivist and absolutist Christian claims about Jesus. I agree that the most prevalent forms of Christianity through the centuries have made such claims, and that they are (in Rita Gross's language) "dangerous, destructive, and degraded." But prevalent as these claims have been, I do not think they are intrinsic or necessary to Christianity.

To explain this statement, I will comment about Rita Gross's essay, which develops the relevant issues at greatest length. As a Christian and occasional theologian, I agree with her at virtually every point. I affirm the approach to religious teachings that she so ably advocates. I agree with her goal: "a theory and praxis of religious pluralism that is neither relativistic nor universalistic, [and] that encourages both commitment to one tradition and appreciation of other traditions." With her, I see verbal and conceptual formulations as pointers to extraverbal truth and not as doctrines to be believed. I affirm that myths and symbols are poetic and metaphorical and not to be understood as historically factual. And all of these insights shape my vision of Christianity.

To turn specifically to Jesus, I begin with negations followed by affirmations. As a Christian, I do not think Jesus is the only way. He is neither indispensable for salvation, nor unique (except in the sense that every person is unique).[8] The exalted terms with which he is spoken of in the New Testament (as messiah, son of God, Lord, Word of God, Wisdom of God, light of the world, bread of life, and so forth) are not literal doctrinal truths but are all metaphors pointing to what Jesus became in the experience and tradition of the early Christian movement.

Positively, cumulatively, and most compactly, I describe the Christian significance of such language about Jesus as follows: Jesus is for us as Christians the decisive manifestation of the sacred. More fully, the classic Christian affirmation about Jesus is twofold: as "true God" and "true human," we see in him most clearly what God is like and what a life full of God is like. He is the decisive disclosure (or revelation) of both.

Decisive does not mean "only." As Christians, we can make this affirmation without saying that Jesus is the only such disclosure, or the only adequate one, or even the most superior one. Rather, we are speaking of who Jesus is *for us*. That is, this affirmation is constitutive of Christian identity, not indispensable for salvation. Christians are people who see the decisive revelation of the sacred *in Jesus,* just as Muslims see it in the Koran, Jews see it in the Torah, and so forth. It is what makes us Christian and not something else. Affirming that Jesus is for us the decisive revelation of God does not require saying that Christianity is the only true religion.

As a Christian, I thus affirm a nonabsolutist, nonexclusivist, nondoctrinal, and nonliteral understanding of Christian scripture and tradition. My affirmation of such a position would be without significance if it were only me and perhaps a few other professors of religious studies who thought this way. Instead, I would argue that this way of seeing has roots in the Christian tradition, notably among the mystics. Like mystics generally, Christian mystics have spoken of the penultimate character of all concepts and language. They know the relativity of all of our categories. They know that being Christian is not about believing correct teachings now for the sake of heaven later but about experiencing God in the present and being transformed by that experience.

Moreover, there is reason to think that we are living in a time when many Christians are beginning to let go of exclusivist and absolutist claims. Based on my experience as an author and lecturer advocating this kind of Christianity, I am convinced that there are millions of mainline Christians in North America for whom the statement that Christianity is *not* the only true religion is good news. It is good news because they have been unable to accept the claim that Christianity is the only way of salvation and have thought that this inability makes them less than Christian. But they find that they can take Christianity seriously when it sees itself as one of the world's great religions—as one cultural-linguistic response to the experience of the sacred.

I do not want to be a Pollyanna about this. In all likelihood, a majority of Christians in North America continue to see Christianity as the only true religion, or at least think they should. Even within mainline denominations, there is resistance among some to "demoting" Christianity.

But a major revisioning of Christianity is occurring among significant segments of the population. Perhaps this is the most important development for Christian involvement in interreligious dialogue: a willingness (indeed, an eagerness) among many mainline Christians to see Christianity, along with the other great religions, as a relative historical construction whose purpose is to mediate the sacred.

NOTES

1. For my most recent treatment, see Marcus Borg and N. Thomas Wright, *The Meaning of Jesus: Two visions* (San Francisco: HarperSanFrancisco, 1998). For earlier treatments, see *Jesus: A New Vision* (1987) and *Meeting Jesus Again for the First Time* (1994), also published by HarperSanFrancisco.

2. I accept the historicity of Jesus as a paranormal healer, even as I think there are limits to "the spectacular."

3. For fuller treatments, see my *Jesus: A New Vision,* pp. 97–124, and *Meeting Jesus Again,* pp. 69–95; and *Jesus and Buddha: The Parallel Sayings,* ed. by Marcus Borg and Ray Riegert (Berkeley: Ulysses Press, 1997), pp. v–xvii.

4. I see the same spiritual-psychological process in central figures in the early Christian movement. Both Paul and the author of John use language of dying and being reborn as a metaphor for this internal process of transformation.

5. Bokin Kim's understanding of "complete" or "radical" faith as involving "immediate contact with God" and "going beyond one's ego boundary" fits well with my reading of the wisdom teaching of Jesus as a Jewish mystic (and with Paul as a mystic, for that matter).

6. A difference: Jesus did not systematize his wisdom teaching; there is nothing equivalent to the Buddha's four noble truths and eightfold path. There may be more than one reason he didn't. Perhaps Jesus' mind did not work that way. Moreover, the brevity of his activity may be a factor; had he lived and taught several more decades, perhaps he would have systematized his understanding of the way.

7. Over time, the metaphor lost its subversive meaning when it became a doctrine to be believed in a religion that began to claim that it had an institutional monopoly on access to God. We Christians initially metaphorized our history, and then we historicized and literalized our metaphors. Or, to make the same point only slightly differently: we mythologized our history, and then we historicized and literalized our mythology.

8. I do think Jesus was an extraordinary human being. Indeed, I regularly speak of Jesus and the Buddha as the two most remarkable figures of religious history.

Exclusivity and Particularity

JOHN DOMINIC CROSSAN

DePaul University

SEVERAL OF THE authors spoke of the imperial exclusivity so characteristic of Christianity. For José Ignacio Cabezón, "What Buddhists find objectionable is (a) the Christian characterization of the deity whose manifestation Jesus is said to be, and (b) the claim that Jesus is unique in being such a manifestation." For Bokin Kim, "most Christians hold to an exclusive view of Christ that claims his uniqueness." For Rita Gross, "the exclusive claims made on behalf of Jesus by Christians appalled me even as a teenager, and my repugnance for exclusive truth claims on the part of religions—any religion—has not diminished since. Thus, part of my journey is working out both a theory and a praxis of religious pluralism that is neither relativistic nor universalistic, that encourages both commitment to one tradition and appreciation of other traditions." I myself find such exclusivistic claims for Christianity, or any other religion, insulting in theory and lethal in practice, objectionable in history and obscene in theology. They are implicitly genocidal even if political impotence limits the divine ethnic cleansing they imagine. But how, as Gross repeats, does one establish "a position that is neither relativistic nor exclusivistic"? My own answer is particularity, but I must explain that in terms of my understanding of Trinity, divinity, and particularity.

Trinity seems a particularly and peculiarly Christian understanding of God, but my proposal is that the structure of the Holy is Trinitarian in all religions that I know about and even in all those I can imagine. I speak very deliberately about the Holy (not about God) as the infinite mystery that surrounds and supports, fascinates and terrifies us. It is that against which we interact as meaning-seeking beings. Be it absolute open meaninglessness or absolute univocal meaning, our interaction with it does not seem to be an option but a necessity. And my point is that the Holy is Trinitarian in structure. It is not just on the one hand that religion is Trinitarian in structure. But it is not on the other hand that the Holy in itself and apart from us is Trinitarian in structure. It is, I propose, that the Holy *in itself as seen by us* across the spectrum of world religious experience is Trinitarian in structure. That Trinity involves, first, *ultimate metaphor,* that foundational image that imagines the Holy as, for example, power, person, state, or order, as nature, god/goddess, nirvana, or mandate of heaven. It involves, second, *material manifestation,* some physical object in which that metaphorical vision is peculiarly, specially, or even uniquely incarnated, some person, place, or thing, some individual or collectivity, some cave or shrine or temple, some clearing in the forest or tree in the desert where that ultimate referent is encountered and experienced. It involves, finally, *preliminary preparation,* for there must be at least one believer to begin with and eventually more to end with. But, as there are always nonbelievers as well, some prior affinity must exist, as it were, between *this* metaphor rather than that, *this* manifestation rather than that, and *this* believer rather than that. For me, therefore, all faith and all religion, not just my own Christianity, is Trinitarian in structure and that structure seems to inhere in the Holy itself, at least insofar as we can see it. For me, therefore, Christianity and Buddhism differ most profoundly on their ultimate metaphor for the Holy: it is person (God) for the former but state (nirvana) for the latter. In Christianity, of course, our ultimate metaphor is rather overinvested: it is person; and that person is parent; and that parent is father. But I leave those specifications aside for the moment.

Divinity is the term I use for any *material manifestation.* By calling such manifestations divine I mean precisely that a religion's ultimate metaphor is experienced by believers as peculiarly, specially, or even uniquely present in that physical phenomenon. In that sense I understand both Christ *and* the Buddha to be divine in exactly the same way—that is, as incarnations of the Holy but within different ultimate metaphors. Christ did not have a monopoly on the Kingdom of God but invited others to enter it just as he had done.

So just as there is the Buddha and the bodhisattva, there is also the Christ and the "Christisattva." And just as the Buddha does not negate the bodhisattva, so neither does the "Christisattva" negate the Christ. It is, in all cases, a question of lived lives and, sometimes, however unfortunately, of accepted martyrdoms. But those last words emphasize a crucial difference between the Christ and the Buddha, and José Ignacio Cabezón underlined it in his article: "Unlike Jesus, the Buddha was not a peasant; his followers seem to have been principally middle- and upper-middle-class men and women, as was his principal audience; and his criticisms were primarily directed at the Brahminical religious beliefs and practices prevalent in his day, not at the social structures that marginalized and oppressed men and women in Ancient India. . . . The Buddha opened up the religious life (and therefore the possibility of salvation) to members of society that had hitherto been denied it: members of the lowest castes and women especially. . . . Nonetheless, as a program of social reform, Jesus' must be recognized as being the more radical and far-reaching, and this no doubt is why the Christian tradition to this day, even when impeded by its own institutional forms, has been at the forefront of social transformation." In this response I focus only on exclusivity and particularity, but this is another major focus for Buddhist-Christian discussion. It is the question of the divergent social class of the Christ and the Buddha. It is the question of the difference between justice and compassion. It is the question of suffering outside the palace created from inside the palace itself. But, for here and now, I leave those questions aside to return to those terms I used twice already, "peculiarly, specially, or even uniquely present," terms that I sum up by the word *particularity.*

Particularity is, for me, the most universal aspect of our humanity. It is what rules us whenever we touch on anything most precious, personal, or profound. Examples may help. Suppose I awoke tomorrow morning beside my wife Sarah and announced, "If I had not met you, fallen in love with you, and married you, I would probably have met, loved, and married someone else and be waking up next to them this morning." That is, of course, a very bad way to start the day. But it is both absolutely true and absolutely inhuman. If it is true, then why is it most imprudent to start the day with its announcement? Particularity is the answer. One experiences and must experience a beloved spouse as "peculiarly, specially, or even uniquely" destined for that relationship and not as an interchangeable cog in a relational machine. As with human love, so it is also—and even more profoundly—with divine faith. It *must* be experienced as "peculiarly, specially, or even uniquely" right, true, valid, and correct. In anything that is of supreme importance to us, be it spouse or family, hobby or passion, job or profession, language or country, there is an inevitable slippage from *a* to *the*. But out of the corner of our minds we recognize that *a* has become *the,* and we know that this is perfectly human and presents no problem—unless it is taken literally and the equally relative absolutes of others are negated. So it is, also or especially, with one's faith or one's religion. It must be experienced as the manifestation of the Holy, but we must never forget or deny that it is actually a manifestation for me and *for us.* To be human is to live in *a* as *the;* to be inhuman is to deny that necessary slippage.

GAUTAMA THE BUDDHA
THROUGH CHRISTIAN EYES

My Unfinished Business with the Buddha

ELIZABETH J. HARRIS
Methodist Church of England

IT WAS IN Sri Lanka in 1984 that I had my first "encounter" with the Buddha. When at the ancient city of Anuradhapura, I stole away from the group I was with to return for a few minutes to the shrine room adjacent to the sacred bo tree, the one believed to have grown from a cutting of the original tree under which the Buddha gained enlightenment. Devotees dressed in white were sitting or prostrating silently. I joined them and looked toward the image, which showed the Buddha sitting in meditation against a painted scene of pale blue sky, white clouds, and mountains. Suddenly the image became more than mere plaster. All I can say is that it communicated. It beckoned. Against the blue of the sky, the serene head became suffused with cosmic significance. I know that there was unfinished business between me and the Buddha.

The moment was prophetic. Two years later, I returned to Sri Lanka to study Buddhism and stayed over seven years. *Study* is not quite the right word because, together with the academic, I also sought to immerse myself in Buddhism with the wish to see it through the eyes of Buddhists. I practiced meditation under Buddhist teachers, participated in temple devotion, and joined pilgrimages. It was a process that meant temporarily letting go of much that was dear to me as a Christian. But the rewards were inestimable. Never again has the image at Anuradhapura "spoken" to me. In fact, on return visits it has appeared artistically poor, certainly no match for the older stone images, open to the air, in other parts of the city. But then, around and inside that very shrine room in May 1985, Tamil guerrillas gunned down 146 innocent devotees, rupturing centuries of devotion with pools of blood.

My seven and a half years in Sri Lanka make it almost impossible for me to write about the Buddha as a complete outsider. I remain a Christian, but the Buddha has become part of me. An exquisitely carved wooden image of the Buddha in meditation is now part of my home. The peace that emanates from it gives me strength. In complete honesty, I can say that I revere the Buddha.

But what Buddha do I revere? Do I revere the Buddha in the same way as Buddhists? To reflect on how my appreciation of the Buddha may be different from that of Buddhists is not easy, for Buddhism contains within itself so many faces of the Buddha. There is the historical Buddha of the earlier parts of the Pali canon, the Buddha of the later hagiographic biographies, the Buddha of popular devotion, Mahayana Buddhism's vision of multiple Buddhas and cosmic buddhahood, the Buddha of what has been termed Protestant Buddhism. Yet I sense that there is a common thread within all of these faces—namely, the Lord Buddha as the supreme embodiment of compassion and wisdom, the one who has seen into the nature of reality and the human predicament and has taught the path of liberation.

All that I know of Buddhism tells me that the person of the Buddha is central. The devotion shown to the image is more than would be given to a human teacher and more than would be given to a god. *Acchariya manussa* is one phrase used in the Pali texts—"wonderful man." He is human, yet more than human in that he was enlightened and worked toward this enlightenment without outside aid through countless lives of self-sacrifice and virtue. This I believe all Buddhists would agree to, and such a being is supremely worthy of reverence.

How does my appreciation tally with this? It is the Theravada tradition that has nurtured my own understanding, and it has done so in three ways. First, there has been my reading of the *Sutta Pitaka* of the Pali canon. In the first two years of my time in Sri Lanka, I read through most of the *nikaya* of the *Sutta Pitaka,* albeit in translation, and I found myself encountering again and again a teacher I could respect and revere. "How absolutely right!" frequently came to my lips when I read the discourses. Although it can be argued that the dynamic of the oral tradition conditioned the texts in such a way that it cannot be assumed what is now read are the words of the Buddha, my experience was that a person emerged from my reading—a down-to-earth, practical, compassionate person, who met people where they were and yet pushed their thought forward in devastatingly effective ways through appealing to their experience of reason. For me, a person shone through the message as much as the message itself cast light around the person.

I brought to my encounter with Buddhism both an interest in the contemplative tradition of Christianity and a commitment to social action. I found the words of the Buddha as given in the Pali texts spoke to both of these. One message that leapt out at me from the Buddha through the texts was, "The way you see the world is wrong. Change." At every level, Buddha was in dialogue with the philosophies and thought patterns of his time: deeds, not birth as a criteria for judging humans; action, not withdrawal from action; diligent mental culture to transform the mind rather than ritual; questioning and discernment rather than blind faith—all this the texts show him affirming, and it appealed to me. For instance, in the *Sigalovada Sutta* of the *Digha Nikaya* (DN iii 180ff), the Buddha meets Sigala, prostrating to the quarters of the earth as his relations had always done, his hair wet in the early morning. He cannot give an explanation for his action. The Buddha's response is to stress that to assure right relationships—between parents and children, wife and husband, employer and employee—is the best way to pay homage to the quarters of the earth, an answer rooted in concern that society should be harmonious and governed by both rights and duties. Then, in the *Samanamandika Sutta* (*Majjhima Nikaya* II 22FF), a wanderer puts before the Buddha the view that the most virtuous person is one who does no evil with his body, speaks no evil, and intends no evil. "Then," the Buddha replies, "the most virtuous and spiritually advanced person would be a baby boy lying on its back." Effort to develop wholesome qualities and wholesome action is necessary—not simply refraining from wrong, the Buddha insists.

This practical, eminently sensible teaching spoke with the ring of truth to me. So did the picture repeatedly given by the Buddha of the consequences of ignorance and not-knowing; in other words, a world enmeshed and on fire with selfish craving, destroying harmony, and generating suffering. This accorded very well with my own analysis of the roots of global inequalities and violence.

The Buddha's encouragement of women also spoke to me through the texts. It is true that he is shown to hesitate when his aunt and foster mother come with a band of followers to request ordination. He then lays down extra rules for the nuns that ensure their subordination to monks. Yet the *Therigatha* (The Songs of the Sisters, *Khuddaka Nikaya*) shows him exhorting women to reach the very highest and implying that some had already done so.

The second way in which I have learned of the Buddha is through iconography, art, and devotion. I can remember a Christian priest once said something like this to me: "The Buddha image speaks to me of coldness, of noninvolvement, of a turning away from life. I prefer the image of Jesus Christ with his robes dirty, with the sweat of the poor." I can see why this was said but cannot empathize with it. Traditional Buddhist iconography does present the Buddha as detached, but my contact with text and tradition convinces me it is detachment from those qualities that cause havoc in society, not from concern for human suffering. Within a BBC World Service *Words of Faith,* a four-minute daily talk, I once made this comment on the sense of peace that emanates from the gigantic stone images of the Buddha at the Gal Vihara at Polonnaruwa in Sri Lanka: "It is not the peace of indifference or apathy. It is the peace of wisdom and compassion, which arises when the heart-rending nature of human violence and human greed is fully realized. It is not an anguished, twisted scream of horror at the nature of the world's inhumanity, but a silent, gentle embodiment in stone of empathy, compassion, and strength."

This is what I see in the Buddha image. I sense it is what many Buddhists also see, and it is a source of strength. The *Jataka* or birth stories within the *Khuddaka Nikaya* of the Pali canon show the Buddha to be giving his body, his eyes, his blood, his limbs again and again for the good of others. This perpetuation comes to fruition when he is born as Prince Siddartha, and it is the fruit of this that the image conveys and devotion affirms. "Do not sink yourself in ego-centered anxiety, in frenzied activity and mental turmoil—relax, be mindful, accept that you will age and die, and develop compassion for all that lives." This is the message that seems to come from the image to me.

The third way in which I have learned of the Buddha is through the words of Buddhist friends. "What does the person of the Buddha mean to you?" was a question I asked many Buddhists in Asia and Britain when I was involved in making a series of radio programs on Buddhism. For some the Buddha was supremely a shower of the way, a wise, compassionate teacher, epitome of all that is good. Others went further and spoke of a much more personal sense of inspiration from the example of the Buddha's life. Yet others spoke of realizing enlightenment themselves. One senior Buddhist monk in Sri Lanka said this: "I like to have my Buddha living within me. His enlightenment was personal to him, but as the Mahayanists or Zen Buddhists would say, there's enlightenment in every grain of sand. Why not within me? So I've already got a pacesetter, the Buddha, in my heart so that it keeps inspiring me all of the time."

Such witness has warmed and thrilled me. It does not cause me difficulty as a Christian. I too gain inspiration from the Buddha and hope that his compassion and wisdom will permeate my mind and heart. Yet as a Christian there are inevitably differences in the way I see the Buddha and the way Buddhists do. For, alongside the Buddha, I place Jesus of Nazareth and his relationship with God. I can draw into myself the Buddha's urgent message about the destructive consequences of egocentric craving based on the illusion that there is permanence in our bodies, our possessions, or our happinesses. I can benefit from the practice of mindfulness upon which the Buddha laid so much stress. Yet I have to ask, "Do I believe the Buddha discovered the whole truth about human existence?" If I did, surely I would be a Buddhist. I am not. My encounter with the Buddha and what he taught has changed me irrevocably, but it has not destroyed my belief that there is other power and such a thing as the grace of God.

As I talk to Christians about the Buddha, reactions vary. At one extreme, there are those who see the Buddha image as an idol and Buddhism itself as a cult. At one meeting I addressed, horror was expressed by some listeners when I said I used Buddhist methods of meditation. They believed I was dabbling in the cultic. There can be no doubt that some Christians have no empathy with the Buddha whatsoever, and this is reinforced by material published and broadcast by some conservative evangelical groups. Then at the other extreme are those who would call themselves Christian Buddhists, often through a close encounter with Zen. I am a member of a Buddhist-Christian dialogue group in which there has been deep mutual exploration and a high level of sympathy and understanding. At one weekend retreat at a Buddhist monastery, the shrine room was transformed by the placing of a Christian altar with an icon at the same level as the Buddha image. It was difficult to tell who was Buddhist and who was Christian as we entered, as most of us bowed to both images. In the middle ground are people like the priest I have quoted who have trouble with the concept of detachment in Buddhism and see the Buddha image as embodying an escapist or individualistic spirituality. In this case, dialogue can help to destroy misconceptions. Yet the strength of this view among Christians should not be underestimated, and it is compounded by the hijacking of the Buddha image by some New Age spiritualities.

My personal conviction is that the Buddha has a message for the whole of humankind, not only those who label themselves Buddhist. I do not believe that one has to be a Buddhist to revere the Buddha. The qualities of the Buddha resonate with those of other great religious leaders, whether Jesus, Guru Nanak, or Mahavira. There is a family likeness and this must be recognized and celebrated. But, of course, there are differences. The issue of divinity is just one. These should neither be voided nor seen as inescapably confrontational. For it is at these points of difference that potentially there is the most opportunity for growth. The apparent depth of difference can be proportional to the depth of the potential for mutual enrichment.

Images of the Buddha

Terry C. Muck

Austin Presbyterian Theological Seminary

WHEN I THINK of the Buddha, the subject of my scholarly study, the picture my mind produces is soft and blurred at the edges—out of focus but not in a way that makes it difficult to see or understand. It is more in the way a photography studio uses background and light to project the subject forward. The Buddha, in my mind's eye, seems friendly, accessible. This Buddha, my Buddha, manages to combine great warmth and great mystery.

By contrast, when I think of Jesus, the object of my faith, I see clearly a well-defined personality. There is no portraiture here. It is more like a candid snapshot taken by a very good camera with plenty of natural light; a great photograph, a picture that produces a clear image, in my mind at least, of a person I know and understand. It is a picture of someone walking around Palestine doing great deeds, a father to my Buddha brother—and to me.

I love both the Buddha and Jesus. I have loved Jesus since early Sunday school days in Huntington, Indiana, at the Bible Baptist Church on Lake Street. I have loved the Buddha since I first began reading about him in graduate school at Northwestern University and listening to Walpola Rahula lecture about him in classes there. Both the Buddha and Jesus were great men, doing divine things that have changed the world for billions after them. The differences my mind produces are in the realm of qualities. I love them both, but I see them differently.

Why the differences? I suppose one reason is that *they* are different. Gautama Buddha lived in sixth-century B.C.E. India where he was the son of a king, chose a life of religious itinerancy, and died of food poisoning at eighty years of age. Jesus lived in Palestine in the first century C.E. where he was the son of a carpenter, chose a life of religious itinerancy, and was crucified by the Roman authorities after being convicted on a charge of political subversion.

They both chose a life of religious itinerancy, to be sure. But the meaning of each of those traveling lives has been the subject of great debate, both within and without their respective religious traditions. Disagreements abound. In fact, in one of those odd quirks of human cantankerousness, the deeper one gets into each of the traditions, Buddhism and Christianity, the more diverse and passionate are the views about the Buddha and the Christ.

The diversity of views deep within each tradition can be stunning to the average Buddhist and Christian on the street, who tend to have a rather homogenized view of each other—kind of a standard life story that could be easily summarized in the pages and pictures of a comic book. But deep within the traditions, Buddhists argue about Buddha nature, Buddha veneration, and the role the Buddha plays in human liberation. Christians argue about Jesus' divine and human status, his uniqueness, and the role he plays in human salvation. One good thing about all this disagreement: it makes my musings about the Buddha and Jesus pale in comparison.

Still, I would like to understand better. Why do I see the Buddha and Jesus differently?

SOCIALIZATION AND HISTORY

SURELY THE MOST important reason can be summarized in one word: socialization. I was raised to love Jesus, to believe in him. Here's how I was raised to see Jesus: Jesus is God's son, born to a woman named Mary and a man named Joseph. God sent Jesus to help human beings lost in a morass of bad deeds, psychological confusion, and social injustices. This melange of evil is so pervasive among human beings that solutions can only come from someone outside the system, willing to enter into the system and guide others out, both by what he says and by what he does—how he lives his life.

What Jesus said, what Jesus did, and who Jesus was—all are unique. Others of us can try to live like Jesus—indeed, we should. But none of us, not one, can be Jesus. As a child, I had an image of this in my mind. I used to think of God in heaven making different human beings in a laboratory—kind of the ultimate Santa Claus in his toy shop. And when God made Jesus, he was so good, so perfect, God decided to never make another one—God broke the mold. It may not be very good Christian theology, to be sure, but a good image for a child.

Given this way of seeing Jesus, it is no wonder that I see the Buddha and Jesus differently. It is no wonder that I feel about them differently. I learned about the Buddha by relating the facts and impact of his life—a great religious leader—to the concept in my mind and experience closest to that: my understandings of Jesus. The Buddha was both like Jesus and different from Jesus. Both my mind and my instincts told me they were in the same category. But both my mind and my instincts told me they were different.

My scholarly studies confirmed my spiritual instincts. The Buddha was different. Official Christian dogma teaches that Jesus was divine, a part of the Trinity, three gods in one: Father, Son, and Holy Spirit. Buddhist teachings dogmatize a different understanding of the Buddha—that he was human through and through. The Buddha, as a fellow human, teaches us the way to live life so that our problems can be overcome. Jesus taught us a way to live life that bears witness to the fact that Jesus, as God, has saved us from our sins. The Buddha shows us the way, Jesus is the Way.

The "ways" are remarkably similar. The Noble Eightfold Path is barely distinguishable from the life Jesus described in the Sermon on the Mount. But the Buddha as the Guide and Jesus as the Savior play different roles in *revealing* the Path (the Buddha's role) and *being* the Path (Jesus' role). I'm not making judgments here. I am trying to describe the two teachings—Buddhism and Christianity—in ways that are faithful to the way Buddhists and Christians understand their own traditions.

I am trying to be faithful here, because my experience has taught me a great irony about these teachings. The irony is this: when these teachings actually get worked out in the lives of everyday Buddhists and Christians, something that amounts almost to a role reversal takes place. Let me explain.

THE IRONY

THE IRONY CAN be stated as follows: the popular Buddhist approach to the Buddha tends to produce a godlike Buddha in a religious tradition that insists on his humanity, and the popular Christian approach to Jesus tends to produce a very human Jesus in a religious tradition that insists on Jesus' divinity. It is almost as if the populace has decided to emphasize what the buddhologians and theologians have decreed secondary. The evidence for this reversal is everywhere.

Look back at the first few paragraphs of this essay. In referring to the two founders, I have chosen to most often refer to them as the Buddha and Jesus. In my mind these are the most popular designations of the two men. To be accurate, however, I should choose to refer to them either as the Buddha and the Christ (both honorific titles), as Gautama and Jesus (their given names), or get formal and use Gautama Buddha and Jesus Christ (or Gautama the Buddha and Jesus the Christ). That I don't, and that most Buddhists and Christians on the street would not (as I said, most think in terms of Buddha and Jesus), I think indicates the emphases of popular religiosity.

Or look at what historically happened to the person of the Buddha as the dharma spread from its cultural roots in India and Southeast Asia to China, Japan, Korea, Tibet, and the West. Buddha images became far more elaborate, incorporating the elements of iconography normally reserved for deities, the personalities of far more historical Buddhas became important in a pantheon of Buddhahood, and the role of the Buddha expanded from Guide to God—almost. The line against divinization may have held doctrinally, but perhaps not in the popular mind.

Correspondingly, after the early formal Christian councils that once and for all fixed Jesus' divine status as far as creed and catechism go, the popular Jesus spread from culture to culture as a friend of the people—for example, the Jesus of popular American evangelicalism, the Jesus of Warner Sallman's painting, *Head of Christ,* the dying Jesus of American hymnody such as "The Old Rugged Cross," the word pictures of devotional piety such as Charles Sheldon's *In His Steps,* or the Latin American revolutionary Jesus fighting shoulder to shoulder with the oppressed—a very human Jesus.

It is not that there is anything inherently wrong with this. Both traditions' teachings about their founders are complex enough to handle a great deal of dissonance between institutional doctrine and popular practice. But in order to understand the way I, as a Christian, feel about the Buddha, I find myself compelled to take into account the way I hear others talking about him. I realize that I have been influenced by both "official" Buddhism in my scholarly studies and by popular Buddhism when I lived for two years in the Buddhist culture of Sri Lanka.

Any vision I have of the Buddha is influenced by both these influences and by my Christian background. In attempting to articulate my views of the Buddha, I am driven to that most academic of exercises: breaking down my views of the Buddha into three segments and then attempting to put them back together again into some kind of unitary view.

The "Theological" Buddha

I DON'T CLAIM that a scholarly, academic, and theological view of the Buddha is the most important, but I think it is very important—to me personally, at least. As I mentioned, my first views of the Buddha were mediated by my professor at Northwestern University, Walpola Rahula, a Sri Lankan Buddhist and scholar of unusual gifts. Dr. Rahula began every semester, no matter what area of Buddhism we were to explore, by telling the story of the Buddha and the early Buddhist councils.

This "telling of the story" was eagerly anticipated by my fellow graduate students and I. We made some lighthearted jokes about it, as I remember: "I guess we know what the first lecture will be on—Buddhaghosa and the Pali Scholastic Tradition," we would say. But we were all there on the first day of class to listen to what we already knew well. Dr. Rahula's telling of the story was inspired. There was a depth to the story, a mystery made of an overabundance of meaning, that made the "telling of the story" a formative event for those of us who would go on to be scholars of Buddhism.

Don't misunderstand. Dr. Rahula never abandoned his rigorous canons of scholarship to become a *dhatu*—an advocate for Buddhism. He told the facts as facts, the myths as myths. He included every pertinent scholarly controversy and a few of his own in the recital. But even as he did this, he managed to communicate a love and respect for a great religious leader—his religious leader—that enriched our understanding of Buddhism.

Scholarship surrounding the person of the Buddha has its share of controversies. The researches into the historical Buddha rival those of the search for Jesus. That the Buddha actually existed is a relatively well established historical fact (although questioning of his existence is occasionally done). His birth and death dates are debated —there is no consensus. The words of his teachings recorded in the Pali, Sanskrit, and Chinese canons are surely edited and amended, and some attempts have been made to recover a core.

But—and here is the key point—when compared to the heat and passion with which comparable issues are debated in Jesus research, the Buddhist researchers seem remarkably laid-back about all this. This is not because buddhologians are less rigorous or less devoted to their task. It is because the Buddha occupies a different place on the Buddhist theological spectrum than Jesus does on the Christian one.

This makes a difference in how I look at the Buddha from a purely academic point of view. The hot passion that often accompanies Jesus studies (witness the Jesus Seminar brouhaha) is transmuted into a deep abiding respect of the kind that only a scholar can have for a significant historical personage. It allows for deeply skeptical examination of issues that somehow do not lead to a lessening of regard for the subject but instead to a deepening regard for genuine accomplishments.

It is true that this regard tends toward the impersonal. Scholars make no apologies for the fact that they are interested in accomplishments, social impact, and historical significance. The difference between veneration of the Buddha and regard for the Buddha is the difference between the confessional Buddhist and the Buddhist scholar. Regard excises a relational dynamic that in other contexts is extremely important. But scholars are often unfairly denigrated by nonscholars in this regard.

My scholarly regard for the Buddha seems to have a certain kind of intellectual passion, if it can be called that, that makes it as significant as the devotee's homage. In some ways it is rarer, harder to come by, certainly more open to revision and abandonment altogether should other evidence become available. But it is real, as long as it exists, real in a way that can create commitment of the highest order. Challenge my regard for the Buddha and you have a fight on your hands.

In thinking about this, I have come to see that my scholarly regard for the Buddha has to do with three things. First, the Buddha was a teacher of religious genius. His four noble truths cut to the essence of human psychological existence. My experience tells me they are true. Their nobility is attested to by their effect on hundreds of Buddhists and Buddhist cultures around the world, thriving cultures that are better for having such a comprehensive philosophy as their foundation. As a historian of religions, I study religious systems. By any of my scholarly standards, Buddhism excels. The Buddha changed history.

Second, the Buddha was a social reformer of great subtlety. He was born a Hindu and never really abandoned the general Hindu metaphysic of samsara, dharma, karma: rebirths determined by fulfilling duty according to an ethical-religious standard. Yet he saw some of the injustices of caste and addressed them not by explicitly disavowing caste, but by spiritualizing duty. He managed to still respect some of the social prerogatives of higher castes even as he made available to the lower castes the possibility of spiritual advancement. The Buddha helped reform Indian culture.

Third, the Buddha was pastoral. A woman came to him with a dead child in her arms. She had been carrying the tiny, rotting corpse for days. "Restore my son," she pleaded. The Buddha did not theologize or relativize or refer. He said, "Of course. But in order to do it, I must have a bit of mustard seed from a house in the village which death has not visited." By the time the woman had finished her fruitless canvassing of her neighbors' houses, she was ready to bury her burden. The Buddha changed history. He improved cultures. But he did not do so at the expense of his attention to individual want and need.

The Buddha was a great, good man. As a scholar, I respect him deeply.

THE BUDDHA AND MY SPIRITUAL LIFE

WHEN I TEACH Buddhism now to students preparing for Christian ministry, I try to be objective. I have my own version of "telling the story," I suppose. I do not want, by the way I teach Buddhism, to denigrate the Buddha's teaching. But neither do I want to shortchange any other religion, or my own Christianity. To achieve this I attempt to be objective, to relate the history of this religious tradition, the belief structure the Buddha espoused, the way Buddhism is practiced today. I think I am reasonably successful in maintaining scholarly objectivity.

Still, at the end of the class, students tell me on course evaluations that they can tell I have a special feeling for Buddhism, and in some cases they say they can tell I like the Buddha. This is fair enough. My understanding of scholarly objectivity does not mean becoming a reciting automaton devoid of passion, but simply being as transparent as possible about where I am coming from. So, regarding the Buddha, where am I coming from?

There are several things about the Buddha that I like. These don't have to do particularly with scholarly judgments about the Buddha's life and times but more to do with the way he did things. These are personal judgments about style more than substance, although they are not devoid of substance. They are reasons I would have liked to spend time with the Buddha.

I like the Buddha's commitment to exploring with all of his energy the religious path. He wanted to find truth, spiritual truth, and followed that dream with all his energy. I don't like the fact that he left his wife and young son in order to do that. (This always bothers my students, too.) Even after I factor in the cultural conditions (the cultural endorsement of the *sannyasin*, the spiritually homeless path) and the fact that as a rich man from a rich family, Gautama's wife and young son, Rahula, would be well provided for, I see this abandonment as a less than ideal understanding of human relationships.

Strangely, this "weakness" on the Buddha's part makes me respect him all the more. I don't think modern culture (any culture really) has found the symbiotic solution to the puzzle of interlocking commitment to ideals and relational truth. My great biblical heroes suffered from this difficult conundrum also: Abraham and his strange but true devotion to God and Isaac; David and his twin passions for God and Bathsheba; Paul and his missionary zeal for God and apocalyptic living. It is obvious by the Buddha's life that he never really solved this one either, and that relieves me of the pressure of having to solve it, too.

I like the Buddha's commonsense approach to communal living and institutional realities. The Buddha discovered the dharma by adopting the lifestyle of a wandering ascetic. By both his life and teachings, he emphasized that in some form or another we must all discover the way out by ourselves. "*Ehi passiko*," he said. "Come and see" for yourselves whether my teaching is true. But the Buddha was not blind to the fact that his teachings were becoming popular, that an institution, the *Sangha*, was springing up around people who were leaving other more traditional institutions to discover religious truth.

Reading the texts, I have this sense (and it is a sense only) that the role of leader of the *Sangha* might not have been the Buddha's favorite. Yet it seems to me he displayed great genius in coping with the needs of a growing institution. He held regular conversations with troubled monks. He developed a remarkably detailed yet flexible monastic rule to guide the *Sangha*. He was firm without being doctrinaire, maintained standards without sacrificing compassion, allowed a breadth of opinion without losing focus.

I like the Buddha's approach to personal spirituality. I wrote my dissertation on the Buddhist monastic rule, the *Vinaya Pitaka*, 227 rules plus extended commentary on how the *bhikkhu* (monks) were to live in community. In that study, I came to appreciate the Buddha's approach to morality—*sila*. The dissertation earned me my doctorate. The study of *sila* has been a formative influence in my Christian spirituality. Some background is probably necessary to make sense of how that can be.

Buddhaghosa, the great fifth-century C.E. Buddhist systematician, explained the Buddhist religious path by breaking it down into three elements that are both simultaneously practiced yet also somewhat hierarchical in nature. The foundational stage is morality, upon which is built meditative practice (*samadhi*), which eventually leads to wisdom (*panna*). The rules of the *Vinaya Pitaka* form a foundation of morality: do this, don't do that because doing that will either inhibit your personal practice or disrupt the practice of others.

But the genius of the rules is that even though they seem so mundane in so many ways, they never seem to descend to the level of legalisms, of being a pure law code. Perhaps it is the way they are presented in the *Vinaya Pitaka*. They are all illustrated with stories of monks whose experience, insights, or failures were supposedly the occasion for the development of this particular rule. Perhaps it is because the higher goals of meditation and wisdom are never absent from the rules themselves. Whatever the reason, I have found the *Vinaya's* approach to morality extremely helpful.

I grew up in a Christian tradition where morality was extremely important. Yet I rarely chafed under that emphasis on the dos and don'ts of Christian living, while many of my good friends, raised under similar circumstances, found them intolerable, life-warping. I think the reason for the difference is the way my parents taught this Christian morality. They were not less rigorous. But there was a lightheartedness about our observance that never lost sight of the higher goals we were seeking.

I never understood the significance of that lightheartedness (I certainly never saw it embodied in the joyless worship of our church or the stern countenances of my parents' peers) until I read the *Vinaya Pitaka* and gained some understanding of what the Buddha was doing. But there, halfway around the world and many religions away from my beloved Christianity, was an understanding that helped me, eventually, to make sense of my own faith commitments.

THE BUDDHA IMAGE

I HAVE A seven-inch-high bronze statue of the Buddha sitting in the lotus position. The image is a lean one, not a fat, jolly Buddha from a northern climate where that shape might be venerated, but a tropical ideal of a lean ascetic. It has some of the thirty-seven marks of a perfect man—for example, long earlobes and topknot on the head. The artist has managed to render the Buddha's face with a look both peaceful and patrician, which combined seem to give confidence—*saddha*. It is a beautiful statue.

I wonder if I should call it a statue. I have a lot of options. I could with some accuracy call it a monument, memorial, or shrine because idealizing, remembering, and respecting are all part of the total repertoire of responses Buddhists bring to the person of the Buddha. But those words all have a public, political feel to them that —while accurate in reference to a religious figure who had powerful political impact—end up being too shallow.

If I were appreciating my statue made in Thailand for its artistic qualities, I could call it a statuette, figure, or sculpture, references that target size, shape, overall character, and composition. This would not be totally inaccurate either. The physical shape of the Buddha garners a great deal of attention in the Buddhist religious writings, and Eastern artists find great inspiration in trying to portray the Buddha in ways faithful to both scriptural ideal and cultural fashion.

Yet even though those artists provide Buddhists and non-Buddhists alike with much food for thought, the inspiration of making and appreciating good art still falls short of the religious function of the Buddha statue. So I find I like best the religious words used to describe my statue; not idol, of course, which has come to mean something negative all around. But icon, symbol, and image all have very rich meaning when I try to describe my thinking, feeling, and doing about the Buddha.

Icon, of course, is a Christian word that refers to an artistic painting of Jesus, Mary, or a saint. Traditionally, Orthodox Christians have used icons the most. The reason I think it appropriate to describe my Buddha statue, however, is not the art itself (an icon is two dimensional) but the way Orthodox Christians respond to the art. They kiss and venerate icons, and as I understand it, that is what Buddhists do also in reference to the Buddha.

Symbols both refer us to a reality and participate in that reality. This puts a symbol a cut above a word or a picture. A symbol provides us a surfeit of meaning, appropriate to a religious figure or concept that by definition has more meaning than rational thought alone can communicate. My Buddha statue has a surfeit of meaning to it for me.

But I must say that the word I like best to describe my bronze Buddha is *image.* I am not arguing that this is the best word for all Buddha statues and for all Buddhists and non-Buddhists who look at statues of the Buddha. I am just saying that when I think about my personal response to the Buddha, my Buddha statue presents me with an image of the person of the Buddha and what the Buddha did, and that image in the main fires my imagination for what is possible in the religious life.

So much of the religious life these days seems to me to be characterized by a lack of imagination. In my Christian tradition, for example, I see too few of us stepping up to the challenge of what could be done in the world in the name of our faith. Too many of us seem content to artistically describe a vision, or worse, to reduce everything to the politically possible. I suspect my own tradition in this regard is not unlike other traditions.

Occasionally I see glimmers: Mother Theresa in Calcutta, Dr. Rahula in class. But mostly I find myself thirsty for someone to set the crossbar a notch or two higher—just to see if we might be able to jump over. When I look at my Buddha image, I see a man who gave up everything to follow his lust for truth; who never gave up on seeking truth even when it seemed nowhere to be found; who worked tirelessly for the well-being of all. And I look at the Buddha's face, so peaceful and content, in the midst of doing what most of us view as impossible. And I am inspired.

My view of the Buddha? It is one part scholarly respect, one part practical gratitude, one part pure inspiration. I couldn't think more highly of anyone.

Buddha Loves Me! This I Know, for the Dharma Tells Me So

DONALD K. SWEARER

Swarthmore College

INTEND NO disrespect to either the Buddha or the Christ by my rewrite of Anna Bartlett Warner's 1859 Sunday school song, "Jesus Loves Me." That one might construct the Buddha in the image of a loving Jesus may be more startling or offensive to Buddhists (and also to Christians) than the modern, apologetic view of the Buddha as a rational renouncer. Versions of both can be textually justified; however, each is a reification that reflects the bias of the interpreter. Both ignore the complexity of the figure of the Buddha within the varied and diverse traditions of Buddhism. My starting point in the following essay acknowledges this complexity as well as the inevitable limitations of my personal interpretation of the Buddha, necessarily conditioned by my experience. I propose to structure the essay around two polarities—universal/particular and wisdom/compassion—looking first at the Buddha and then briefly reflecting dialogically at the end of each section on the figure of the Christ.

BUDDHA: UNIVERSAL AND PARTICULAR

IN MY PERSONAL experience in Buddhist Asia, especially Thailand, and my studies of Buddhist traditions, in particular the Theravada, I have been impressed by the creative tension between the universal and particular dimensions of the figure of the Buddha. Even the modern Western view of the

Buddha evidences this tension. Typically the word *Buddha* evokes the story of Prince Siddhattha's renunciation of his royal status, subsequent quest for enlightenment, and eventual realization of *nibbana*.[1] In the hands of a comparative mythologist such as Joseph Campbell, the detailed embellishments of the Buddha's sacred biography are absorbed into the tripartite, monomyth structure of the hero's narrative—separation, attainment, return. For Campbell, the story of the historical Buddha, Siddhattha Gotama, represents a rite of passage, a deep psychological truth of self-discovery symbolized by other heroes in world mythology. Despite the antistructuralist critique by historical and textual scholars, as well as the feminist criticism that the heroic journey does not reflect women's experience, in one form or another the Buddha reified as an exemplar of the universal paradigm of the individual's journey of self-realization continues to capture the Western imagination.

A somewhat more sophisticated version of the universal hero motif is the Buddha as "rational renouncer," an interpretation favored by both Buddhists and scholars of Buddhism who portray the Buddha as an empiricist and pragmatist somewhat on the order of William James. In this view, Prince Siddhattha's quest was a rational response to the experience of suffering, and the truth he perceived on the night of his enlightenment was nothing more nor less than a direct perception of the universal law of cause and effect obscured to ordinary awareness. De-emphasizing both the ascetical and devotional aspects of the Buddha's sacred biography, the rational renouncer school of thought places its emphasis on epistemological transformation characterized in Buddhist texts as "seeing things as they really are."

The Buddha as universal hero and as rational renouncer can be critiqued as modernized, rationalized, westernized reifications of the Buddha, an example of the "orientialist" distortion that characterized the colonial project. Charles Hallisey has pointed out that such reconstructions of the Buddha were not merely the products of Western scholars but owed much to Asian Buddhists as well.[2] But are we to assume that throughout the history of Buddhism, similar hermeneutical moves and debates over the nature of the Buddha did not exist? I find a tension in the Buddhist tradition between two contrasting images of the Buddha: as an exemplar of a universal truth, and as a being defined by the contingencies of human particularities.

Theravada Buddhists find strong support in the *sutta* for a humanistic interpretation of the Buddha. In particular, they argue that the Buddha of the early Buddhist canonical texts specifically denied that he was a god, and that he was a teacher of the truth he perceived at his enlightenment. They find support for this view in the *Mahaparinibbana Sutta,* wherein the Buddha tells his followers that when he dies the teaching and the disciplinary rules he promulgated—the dharma and *vinaya*—will be his successor. They also point to the *sutta* passage where the Buddha says, "Whoever sees me sees the *dharma;* whoever sees the *dharma* sees me"[3] to support the position that the dharma overshadows the historical Buddha or that the teachings of the Buddha supersede his person.

Buddhadasa Bhikkhu, one of Thailand's most creative Buddhist thinkers, contends that the statement, "Whoever sees me sees the *dharma*" has implications far beyond a portrayal of the Buddha as a historical person:

> The Buddha in everyday language refers to the historical Enlightened being, Gotama Buddha. It refers to a physical man of flesh and bone who was born in India over two thousand years ago, died, and was cremated. This is the meaning of the Buddha in everyday language. Considered in terms of *dharma* language, however, the word Buddha refers to the Truth that the historical Buddha realized and taught, the *dharma* itself. Now the *dharma* is something intangible, it is not something physical, certainly not flesh and bones. Yet the Buddha said it is one and the same as the Enlightened One. Anyone who fails to see the *dharma* cannot be said to have seen the Enlightened One. The Buddha is one and the same as that truth by which he became the Buddha, and anyone who sees the truth can be said to have seen the true Buddha.[4]

It is equally true that Pali texts support the view that the Buddha was highly revered not simply as a mirror of the dharma but as a being to be venerated, as a source of merit, and even to be worshiped. It is argued, for instance, that the title *Bhagavant* (Blessed One) was more than an honorific, and that following his death the Buddha as an object of devotion formed the basis for the cult of relics and images. To be more precise, one finds in the Buddhist *sutta* what can be characterized as a controversy between the philosophers and the devotees over the nature of the person of the Buddha: whether the Buddha should be seen as the mirror of the dharma or as the subject of devotion whose very body radiates supramundane power. The *Sutta to Prince Bodhi* (*Bodhirajakumara Sutta, Majjhima Nikaya,* no. 85) illustrates this controversy. The good prince invites the Blessed One to his palace in order to pay him homage. As the Buddha approaches the entrance, the prince says, "Venerable sir, let the Blessed One step on the cloth, let the Sublime One step on the cloth, that it may lead to my welfare and happiness for a long time." To this request made thrice, Ananda, the Buddha's chief disciple, replies, "Prince, let the cloth be removed. The Blessed One will not step on a strip of cloth; the Tathāgata has regard for future generations." The text implies conflicting opinions concerning the person of the Buddha, giving precedence to the view that the body of the Buddha is not to be venerated as a source of merit."

The main point is that in Buddhist texts and Buddhist practice, I have found a tension between identifying the Buddha with a universal truth beyond form and image and the various ways of particularizing the person of the Buddha that range from apocryphal texts designed to promote Buddha *bhakti* (devotion) to veneration of the Buddha's bodily relics. Currently I am completing a study of the northern Thai ritual of Buddha image consecration. Attending several of these all-night ceremonies—a ritual reenactment of the night of the Buddha's enlightenment—has been among the most moving experiences of my life. I have been particularly impressed with the ritual's underlying meaning of making the Buddha present as the image effectively becomes the Buddha's surrogate. In doing so the image (*buddharupa* = form of the Buddha) makes the universal dharma present. In particularizing that which is universal, the Tathāgata (a thus-gone-one in lineage of the Enlightened Buddha) becomes the *Bhagavant*—Blessed One. Through the chanting of sacred mantras, the recital of the story of the Buddha's enlightenment, the presence of holy monks, and a night devoted to meditation, the Buddha image consecration ritual transforms the Buddha image into a fusion of the universal dharma and the saint known as the Buddha.

In an earlier book on interreligious dialogue, I pointed to several ways in which my study of Buddhism provided insight into my understanding of

Christianity; for example, how the Buddhist doctrine of not-self (*anatta*) enlarged my comprehension of Paul's claim, "It is no longer I who live but Christ who lives in me."[5] In a similar vein, my attempts to come to terms with the various ways Buddhists have viewed the Buddha through history and currently experience the Buddha in rituals such as the Buddha image consecration ceremony have enlarged my understanding of the paradox of the Incarnation, of God becoming Jesus the Christ, of the universal Logos becoming flesh, of the infinite becoming finite. Though seemingly worlds apart, participating in Buddha image consecration rituals in northern Thailand has given new meaning to Kierkegaard's subtle dialectic I studied nearly forty years earlier, the dialectic of the incarnate God overcoming the dualism of the finite and the infinite and in this fusion transforming the boundaries of ordinary logical thinking that incarcerate the religious imagination. In the expanse of Chiang Rai's Temple of the Emerald Buddha in the far north of Thailand, with the darkness illuminated by altar candles and the silence broken only by the rhythmic chanting of monks seated before newly consecrated Buddha images, it was as though I experienced in the fullness of time not only the instantiation of the universal dharma, but the enfleshment of the universal Logos.

BUDDHA: KNOWLEDGE AND COMPASSION

IN MY STUDY of Buddhism I have encountered another major tension in the way Buddhists experience the Buddha, a polarity between knowledge (*paññā*) and compassion (*karuṇā*). The tension is represented at the very beginning of the legendary life of the Buddha. The well-known story of Siddhartha's renunciation of his family and princely status to search for the supreme knowledge (*nibbana*) that defined his Buddhahood (*sammā-sambuddha*) is taken as the paradigm of Buddhism's valorization of knowledge as the supreme value. Ignorance drives the Wheel of Rebirth (*saṃsāracakka*). Only by overcoming ignorance and mental defilement (*kilesa*) does the Buddha or anyone else realize the wisdom-gone-beyond (*gate gate pāragate bodhi svāhā*).

One has only to read cursorily in the vast corpus of canonical and noncanonical Buddhist literature or observe Buddhist attitudes and behaviors regarding the Buddha to realize that the Tathāgata represents much more than wisdom (*paññā*). For example, in the *Jātaka* literature where the future Buddha appears in a variety of human and animal guises, the Blessed One personifies a wide range of moral and spiritual values, not solely the paradigmatic value of wisdom. The last ten of the 547 Pali canonical tales and their appended commentary represent an amalgam of moral perfections (*parami*) that define the moral prerequisites for Buddhahood. In their various permutations, these virtues—ranging from renunciation and equanimity to patience and loving-kindness—play a major role in all Buddhist traditions. Perhaps best known to Western students of Buddhism are the Mahayana bodhisattva perfections delineated in such texts as Santideva's *Bodhicaryavatara* (Entering the Path of Enlightenment). Above all other characteristics, wisdom and compassion define bodhisattvahood.

Included in the final ten Pali *Jātaka* is the story of Sama, the personification of loving-kindness (*mettā*).[6] It is a tale of self-sacrificial, redemptive love. Sama lives a life of tender, caring devotion to his parents, Dukulaka and Parika, who, while living in the forest as ascetics, are blinded by a poisonous snake. One day King Piliyaka of Benares is hunting in the forest and observes Sama filling a water jar. Nearby, deer are drinking from the same pool, unafraid because Sama embodies loving-kindness toward all living creatures. Thinking that the youth must be a *deva* (god) or *nāga* (a serpent divinity), the king wounds Sama with an arrow so that he will not escape. Sama falls dying to the ground but bears no grudge or hostility toward the king. When Piliyaka learns Sama's identity and that he is the only support for his blind parents, the king is filled with remorse. Vowing to protect and care for Sama's parents, the king goes to tell them of their son's death. The parents, like Sama himself, bear no malice toward the king and ask to be taken to see their son's body. There they make a solemn Act of Truth (*sacca-kiriyā*) while praying by their son's side. As a consequence, the poison is released from Sama's body and he is restored to life. At the same time, through divine intervention, his parents regain their eyesight. Sama then teaches the marveling king the lesson of how *deva* protect those who care for others, in this case his parents, with loving-kindness (*mettā*).

Although compassion and loving-kindness appear to complement wisdom as moral virtues prerequisite to Buddhahood and figure prominently in narrative literature associated with the future Buddha, one also encounters a tension in the tradition between wisdom and compassion. In the canonical story of the Buddha's *nibbana,* following his enlightenment the Blessed One debates whether or not to teach the dharma and share with others the supreme truth he discovered. His affirmative decision is celebrated as a prime example of the Buddha's great compassion (*mahā-karuṇā*).[7]

When he surveys the world following his enlightenment, the Buddha perceives that few people will be able to understand his teaching. Therefore, he deliberates:

> Enough with teaching the Dharma
> That even I found hard to reach;
> For it will never be perceived
> By those who live in lust and hate.

> Those dyed in lust, wrapped in darkness
> Will never discern this abstruse Dharma
> Which goes against the worldly stream,
> Subtle, deep, and difficult to see.

Fortunately, Brahma Sahampati intercedes on behalf of the world by pleading with the Buddha: "The world will be lost, the world will perish, since the mind of the Tathagata, accomplished and fully enlightened, inclines to inaction rather than teaching the Dharma." Upon hearing Brahma's plea, the Blessed One "out of compassion for all beings surveyed the world with the eye of a Buddha" and decided to teach the supreme truth he had attained in his enlightenment. The story demonstrates that although priority is given to the wisdom of enlightenment, the most complete expression of Buddhahood includes the compassion that motivates the Buddha to teach the dharma to a suffering humanity. The Tathāgata's stated mission, that he came to teach the cause of suffering and the way to its cessation, takes on the meaning of an act of cosmic compassion. This story can be seen as an anticipation of the cosmic dimensions of the compassion of the Amida Buddha in the Japanese Pure Land tradition.

The compassion of the Buddha bears a family resemblance to other moral qualities—in particular, empathy (*anukampā*),[8] the ability to identify with the suffering of others (*saṃvega*),[9] the detachment from self-interest that allows one to delight in the joy of another solely for the sake of the other (*muditā*), and to love others nonpreferentially (*upekkhā*). Because these qualities are often associated with both healing and the feminine, it is not surprising that the Buddha assumes both healing and feminine properties. In the *Lotus Sutra*, for example, the Teacher of the dharma is equated with spiritual healing, and other Mahayana sutras celebrate healing Buddhas and bodhisattvas, in particular.[10] In the Tantrayana tradition of Tibet, wisdom and compassion are feminized in the form of Prajñāpāramitā and Tārā and other female divinities often depicted with male counterparts.[11]

From the standpoint of devotional belief and practice, the Buddha's compassion is often understood not only as the power of the Blessed One to release the devotee from the ontological condition of suffering (*dukkha*), but also to protect and intercede directly on behalf of one's welfare or the welfare of others in mundane, practical ways. When a young college student from Chiang Mai visits the Flower Garden Monastery (*Wat Suan Dok*) before her final exam, purchases a small square of gold leaf, and kneeling in prayer applies it to the forehead of one of the Buddha images, she is motivated less by honoring the Buddha than the hope the act will improve her chances of doing well on the exam. In other words, she hopes that the Buddha acting out of enlightened compassion will intercede on her behalf.

Virtually all Buddhist ceremonies have as part of their underlying meaning the purpose of protecting those gathered together for a particular occasion, be it an ordination, funeral, or Sabbath meeting, as well as protecting those not present or deceased. Throughout Theravada Asia—Sri Lanka and mainland Southeast Asia—the primary texts recited at all meritorious (*puñña*) rituals are found in a handbook compiled in Sri Lanka called *Paritta*, meaning "protection." One example included in the collection is the *Angulimala Sutta* (*Majjhima Nikaya*, no. 86). At the Buddha's request, the monk Angulimala vows an Act of Truth that the Blessed One assures the holy monk will guarantee the birth of a healthy child.

The traditional conclusion of merit-making ceremonies in northern Thailand ends with the following recitation by the monks assembled for the meeting:

May all living beings who suffer be free from suffering;
Those who meet with danger be free from danger;
Those who are sorrowful be free from sorrow.
May all divine beings (*deva*) approve
Of the merit we have accumulated;
So that by their power we may gain wealth.
Give generously, observe the precepts faithfully,
Meditate continuously.
May I be protected by the powers of the Buddha,
The *paccekabuddhas,* and the *arahants.*

The words suggest that the compassion of the Buddha refers not only to his teaching about the cause of suffering and the way to its cessation, but also the hope that the Buddha's Act of Truth—an act that defeated the powerful forces of Māra at the Tree of Enlightenment—will protect me and my loved ones in all kinds of circumstances and situations. Indeed, as a sign of that hope, devotees may wear a neck chain from which a Buddha amulet is suspended.

I do not mean to imply that in practice Buddhists in Thailand always resolve the tension between wisdom and compassion on the side of compassion reduced to the Buddha's power to protect or guarantee material success. I have been impressed by the high regard with which Thai Buddhists hold meditation not only in theory but also in practice. To be sure, I know Buddhists who meditate with the same apotropaic intention that informs their merit-making rituals; however, I have observed devotees in village temples meditating with a dedication and quiet intensity that suggests a higher purpose, a quest for the Buddha's "wisdom-gone-beyond."

What about Christianity? Is there a tension between the Christ of wisdom and the Jesus of love? Does the Gospel of John exhibit a tension between the creative power of wisdom set from the beginning of time and the redemptive power of God's love in time and space? And does Paul suggest that true knowledge—not seeing-through-a-glass-darkly knowledge—and universal compassion or agapic love are mutually complimentary, much as are the Buddha's enlightenment and his great compassion? Am I reading the polarity of wisdom and compassion that I see in Buddhism into John and Paul and, by extension, the Christian theological tradition more broadly from Augustine to Sallie McFague? If so, am I Buddhasizing my tradition, or is it rather that my experience of Buddhism has opened up for me new insights and interpretations as I wrestle for personal meaning in my dialogical faith betwixt-and-between Christianity and Buddhism?

I attended a funeral at my home church yesterday. What I heard in scripture and sermon and saw on the faces and in the tears of family and friends was not only the wisdom and love of the universal Christ, but the particular assurance and protection seen in the figure of Jesus surrounded by children framed in the stained glass window by the pulpit. *"Jesus loves me! This I know. . . ."*

NOTES

1. Since my primary referent is to Theravada Buddhism, I have chosen to use Pali rather than Sanskrit spellings, such as *nibbana* instead of nirvana, unless a reference is specifically to Mahayana traditions.

2. Charles Hallisey, "Roads Taken and Not Taken in the Study of Theravada Buddhism," in *Curators of the Buddha: The Study of Buddhism under Colonialism,* ed. Donald S. Lopez Jr. (Berkeley and Los Angeles: University of California Press, 1995), pp. 31–61. For an essay on the Western construction of Indian Buddhism, see Gregory Schopen, "Archaeology and Protestant Presuppositions in the Study of Indian Buddhism," in *Bones, Stones, and Buddhist Monks: Collected Papers on the Archaeology, Epigraphy, and Texts of Monastic Buddhism in India* (Honolulu: University of Hawai'i Press, 1997), pp. 1–22.

3. Presumably the Christian version of the Buddha's claim would be, "Whosoever sees me [Jesus] sees God [the Father]."

4. Buddhadasa Bhikkhu, *Me and Mine: Selected Essays of Bhikkhu Buddhadasa,* ed. Donald K. Swearer (Albany: State University of New York Press, 1989), pp. 127–28. For a fuller discussion of Buddhadasa's interpretation of the Buddha, see Donald K. Swearer, "Bhikkhu Buddhadasa's Interpretation of the Buddha," *Journal of the American Academy of Religion,* 64 no. 2 (Fall 1996), pp. 134–54.

5. Donald K. Swearer, *Dialogue: The Key to Understanding Other Religions* (Philadelphia: Westminster Press, 1977).

6. For a summary of the last ten *Jataka,* see Elizabeth Wray et. al, *The Ten Lives of the Buddha* (New York: Weatherhill, 1972). Included in the volume are color plates of Thai temple murals of the tales. This summary is adapted from Elizabeth Lyons, *The Tosachat in Thai*

Painting, Thailand Culture, New Series, no. 22 (Bangkok: The Fine Arts Department, 1963), pp. 9–11.

7. *Ariyapariyesana Sutta* (The Noble Search). *Majjhima Nikaya,* no. 26. See *The Middle Length Discourses of the Buddha,* trans. Bhikkhu Nanamoli and Bhikkhu Bodhi (Boston: Wisdom, 1995), pp. 253–68.

8. As the Buddha taught the dharma for the benefit of humankind, so should monks be motivated by empathy for the world. *Sangiti Sutta, Digha Nikaya* iii, p. 213.

9. For the linkage of *saṃvega* and acting on behalf of others, see *Sangiti sutta, Digha Nikaya* iii, p. 214.

10. See Raoul Birnbaum, *The Healing Buddha* (Boulder: Shambala, 1979).

11. See Robert A. F. Thurman, *Wisdom and Means: The Sacred Art of Tibet* (New York: Tibet House, 1991).

The Buddha Offered Me a Raft

BONNIE THURSTON

Pittsburgh Theological Seminary

> Es gibt, so glaube ich, in der Tat jenes Ding nicht, das wir "Lernen" nennen.
>
> —Hermann Hesse, *Siddhartha*

I MUST WARN you at the beginning that what follows is an embarrassingly personal reflection—a confession even—and not a scholarly essay. I cannot be dispassionate about the Buddha, to whom in a roundabout way I owe both my status as an ordained Christian minister and perhaps the greatest joy of my life, the study and practice of the Christian scripture. How? In February 1970 I was given a copy of Hesse's novel *Siddhartha,* a fictionalized account of the Buddha's life. Already an active Christian, it was this gift, received my senior year in high school, that introduced me to Buddhism and to the reality of spiritual journey and the possibility of enlightenment. While I know the Buddhist meaning of that term, it serves for Christians as well, because our God could not leave us in darkness but made light the first creature (Gen. 1:1–5) and came among us as light (John 1:1–5).[1] When in the fall of 1970 my brother traveled to Japan, the memento I requested was a small statue of the Buddha. It is beside me as I write. In 1983 when we moved to Germany, the second book I bought in German was *Siddhartha;* the first was the New Testament.

Over the years I have had the opportunity to continue to study the life of the Buddha and the spread and development of his teachings. By *the Buddha,* of course, I mean Sakyamuni ("sage of the Sakyas") Buddha ("enlightened one"), son of Suddhodana and Maya, whom they called Siddhartha ("wish fulfilled" or "goal realized") and whom we also know as Gotama or Gautama (literally "superior cow"), whose dates are given variously as 560–480 B.C. or 460–380 B.C.[2] I am appreciative of what I have learned—applying the root meaning of that word, *appretiare:* "to see" or "to appraise." The Buddha has helped me to see and to appraise or evaluate many aspects of life. The appreciation that follows, then, is both a grateful recognition as of benefits received and a sensitive awareness or an estimate. I have tried both to view the Buddha clearly and to appraise what he has meant in my life. In essence, Buddhism and the Buddha have been for me the means of establishing a personal, internal religious clarity about what I do believe, passionately. In a deeply Buddhist sense, the Buddha has been my raft. But he has not been my Savior.

There is, as Tillich noted in *Christianity and the Encounter with World Religions,* a point "in the depth of every living religion . . . at which the religion itself loses its importance, and that to which it points breaks through its particularity."[3] It has helped me to understand religions as fingers and the Divine Reality as the moon to which they point. And I am convinced that Tillich's breakthrough point is usually reached by means of deep penetration into one religious tradition. Jacques-Albert Cuttat was exactly correct: "The more deeply a person probes into his own religious faith, the more he is able to understand the religious faith of others from the inside; conversely, the more a person explores religious connections other than his own, the more he deepens his understanding of his own religion."[4] This has been my experience. Dialogue with the Buddha has given me great clarity about the Christ. And the study and practice of Christianity has afforded me my glimpses of the moon.

What, then, do I appreciate about the Buddha? What have I learned from him? To help focus my answer, I read or reread a number of different accounts of his life[5] and noted six specific aspects of his life and teaching (his quest itself; his powers of analysis; his pragmatism; his moral vision; his compassion; and the outcome of living, his "way") that have attracted and taught me.

First, I am appreciative of the Buddha's quest itself. To put it simply, according to the accounts of his early life he had it all but realized he had nothing. Many a lesser person has been content with a life of pleasure, safety, and satiety. I stand in awe of the Buddha's devotion to Truth and the hunger for transcendence that led to his Great Renunciation. Second, I appreciate his amazing powers of analysis that made the quest possible. He saw deeply into the nature of things. As Carrithers points out, "the Buddha's laboratory was himself, and he generalized his findings to cover all human beings;" he "depended wholly upon . . . direct personal knowledge, direct personal experience, direct witnessing in the here and now."[6] In light of my own propensity for self-deception, I find the Buddha's self-awareness (I use the term knowing, if not fully understanding, the doctrine of *anatta*) and ability to analyze what he found astonishing.

Third, the Buddha seems fully to have penetrated the realm of human realities. And his pragmatism in facing them has taught me a great deal. The Buddha faced facts. When he experienced the Four Signs, he did not turn away or retreat into the life of luxury offered by his father and his social status; he looked clearly and saw the Signs for what they were, metaphors for the human condition. Quoting Thich Nhat Hanh, Thomas Merton notes: "The basic aim of Buddhism . . . arises out of human experience itself—the experience of suffering—and it seeks to provide a realistic answer to man's most urgent question: how to cope with suffering. The problem of human suffering is insoluble as long as men are prevented by their collective and individual illusions from getting directly to grips with suffering in its very root within themselves."[7]

The Buddha shed illusions and got "directly to grips" with the human reality and described it in the Four Noble Truths. Then he proposed a pragmatic solution to the problem he saw (the Eightfold Path) that avoided the extremes of either asceticism or self-indulgence. The "Via Media," the Middle Way of the Eightfold Path, is a practical prescription for his particular diagnosis of the human condition. The Buddha not only saw the disease clearly; he proposed a cure that most people can undertake.

While the Physician basically prescribed "heal thyself," he never lost sight of the fact that human action has inescapable moral consequences that are both personal and corporate. What I do affects not only me, but others. The Buddha understood that the universe has a fundamental moral order. As one seeks to cure one's own disease, she or he must never lose sight of the effects of a person's actions on others. One's skill in doing so (*kusala*) is also a moral good. "For the Buddha skillfulness cut two ways: its consequences were good for oneself, but good for others as well." For the Buddha "to do good was precisely to act both in one's own *and* in someone else's interest."[8] Again, this is a very practical test of "the good." The high morality of the Buddha's Way overcomes the selfish focus of much that calls itself "contemplative spirituality" in our day. And that leads to my fifth point of appreciation of the Buddha—his great compassion.

Schumann is exactly correct when he writes that "loving-kindness was the essential trait in the Buddha's character."[9] While Buddhist literature contains many examples of it, I especially delight in the story that the little ringlets one sees on the head of the meditating Buddha are not hair, but snails he was too compassionate to disturb. This compassion of the Buddha, which His Holiness the Dalai Lama describes as "undiscriminating, spontaneous, and unlimited compassion for all sentient beings,"[10] springs, I think, from his essential selflessness, his refusal to grasp at a "self." His was the kenotic impulse I find in my own Lord Jesus, who, in the words of St. Paul, "emptied himself" and "humbled himself" (Phil. 2: 7, 8).[11] The Buddha and the Christ are both characterized by generous self-giving[12] and the willingness to share the fruits of their personal enlightenments with all comers. The Buddha's compassion for all beings is heard in his invitation, "Let the doors to Deathlessness be opened to all who are able to hear!"[13] The example of the Buddha's compassion has stretched me and encouraged me to throw open the doors of my own heart to widen the circle of my concern and caring to all of life.

Before noting the final aspect of the Buddha's life and teaching of which I am especially appreciative, let me mention two aspects of his practice that have been enormously helpful, which I have taken home as gifts to be shared in the household of Christianity: meditation and detachment, both of which engender focus and "presence." I am not the only Christian for whom meditation (and the form I have in mind is zazen or "sitting") has been an important discipline and practice. For example, William Johnston's book *Christian Zen* examines how "Zen can teach [Christians] a methodology in prayer."[14]

And sitting has impressed on me a fundamental truth that is expressed this way by Walpola Rahula: "As long as you are conscious of yourself you can never concentrate on anything."[15] Self-forgetfulness is a wonderful liberation that allows us to be fully present to others and to life itself. It partakes of something of the selflessness of the Buddha and of the Christ. (Tillich, in fact, noted that what is particular in Jesus "is that he crucified the particular in himself for the sake of the universal."[16]) Sitting meditation has helped me move beyond my particularity toward Being itself, and, paradoxically, I have found I am most myself when I am least self-conscious.

Shunryu Suzuki has said, "What we call 'I' is just a swinging door which moves when we inhale and when we exhale." He continues, "when we become truly ourselves, we just become a swinging door, and we are purely independent of, and at the same time, dependent upon everything."[17] I think the same idea is expressed from the Christian viewpoint by Thomas Merton, who wrote that "Zen is the very awareness of the dynamism of life living itself in us—aware of itself, in us, as being the one life that lives in all."[18] Sitting has brought me to this awareness and is, itself, a wonderful corrective to the Christian compulsion to "do." It helps me simply to "be" and simply to appreciate being. And it has introduced many of us Christians to similar forms of prayer that are deeply rooted but, alas, often choked out by historical weeds of various kinds in Christian soil. Sitting meditation has brought with it the gift of focus—a wonderful gift indeed.

The second aspect of practice that I lift up—detachment—is really intrinsically related to the second and third of the Buddha's Noble Truths, the truth of the arising of *dukkha* (Pali "suffering," "pain," "sorrow," or "misery"[19] but perhaps most helpfully rendered in English by "unsatisfactoriness") and of its cessation. If I understand him correctly, the Buddha teaches that because we are ignorant of the nature of reality, we "crave" or "thirst for" or "desire." This is a kind of grasping that ties us to a material world that is illusory. To be liberated from *dukkha,* one must cease craving. Put most simply, we must learn to be detached from things, persons, even our sense of self. As I observe it in myself, desire usually projects me into the future, where the things I do not have now and desire exist. Desire prevents me from living in the present moment, the only moment that is and the only one in which I can welcome and receive God. Desire prevents my being at peace with what is.

Understanding detachment as a means of living in the present is an especially helpful point for me as a Christian because, in what is perhaps the most dramatic self-revelation of God in scripture before the Incarnation of Jesus, the call story of Moses in Exod. 3–4, God reveals the divine self as "I AM, YHWH." While I understand that the Hebrew term is variously translated "I AM the one Who IS," emphasizing God's eternal Being, "I AM the One Who causes to Be," emphasizing God's creativity, and, less frequently, "I WILL BE," emphasizing the promise of God's presence, the I-AM-NESS of God suggests that if God is not received or welcomed or found in the now, God is unlikely to be experienced at all. (Perhaps this is why St. Paul tells the Corinthians, "See, now is the acceptable time; see, now is the day of salvation" [2 Cor. 6:2] and, in speaking to the Colossians of the mystery of God, says it "has now been revealed" [Col. 1:26]). The Buddha's teachings on detachment have led me as a Christian not only to freedom in the present moment, but into the Presence of God.

Finally, then, those who have heard of and responded to and lived out the Buddha's path have found a focus and equanimity that is impressive. Again admiring his pragmatism, the coarse (and very un-Buddhist) way to express this appreciation is to say that following the Buddha's path leads to positive results. Seeking the goals of the Buddhist path to liberation, "to act without desire for success, with goodwill toward all, and clearly aware"[20] and to create "an entirely new consciousness which is free to deal with life barehanded and without pretenses,"[21] produces marvelous personal and social outcomes. I am deeply attracted to the Buddhist goal of "living radiantly in the present"[22] and to the Buddha who both did it and demonstrated how to do it. And this is precisely where my problem lies, and what keeps me firmly Christian. I admire and am attracted to the Buddha, but he pushes me away.

This is to say that I personally have not been able to achieve the radical self-sufficiency upon which the Buddha insists. "Be lamps unto yourselves," he says. According to the *Digha Nikaya,* one of the last teachings of the Buddha to Ananda was: "You should live as islands unto yourselves, being your own refuge, seeking no other refuge; with the Dhamma as an island, with the Dhamma as your refuge, seeking no other refuge. . . . Those monks who in my time or afterwards live thus, seeking an island and a refuge in themselves and in the Dhamma and nowhere else, these zealous ones are truly *my* monks and will overcome the darkness (of rebirth)."[23]

While I admire the confidence in the human being that asserts that everyone who strives for emancipation and enlightenment can find it by personal effort, that, alas, does not square with my experience. I strive to be selfless and am, in fact, often full of myself, selfish, and self-deceived. In the words of a famous Christian prayer by Thomas Merton, "The fact that I think that I am following [God's] will does not mean that I am actually doing so."[24]

My experience is less that of the Dhammapada, which notes: "By oneself indeed is evil done and by oneself is one defiled. By oneself is evil left undone and by oneself indeed one is purified. Purity and impurity depend on oneself,"[25] and more that of St. Paul, who lamented, "I do not understand my own actions. For I do not do what I want but I do the very thing I hate" (Rom. 7:15) and "For I do not do the good I want but the evil I do not want is what I do" (Rom. 7:19). The darkness is so great. My candle is so small. Strive as I may, I can't illuminate myself. Again, with Paul I cry out, "Wretched [woman] that I am! Who will rescue me from this body of death? Thanks be to God through Jesus Christ our Lord!" (Rom. 7:24–25)

In the struggle to be a lamp to myself, I am brought face to face with Jesus Christ. There are many points of comparison between the Buddha and the Christ, and many helpful comparisons have been drawn.[26] I want to focus on one that I have not seen: the attitude of each toward his followers. The Buddha says, "Be lamps unto yourselves" and "one is one's own refuge."[27] (At this point it may be clear to the Buddhist reader that I need more instruction in what it means "to take refuge." My understanding is that it means to rely on the example but not the person of the Buddha. But I stand ready to be corrected.) The Christ says, "Come to me, all you that are weary and are carrying heavy burdens, and I will give you rest" (Matt. 11:28) and "I am the light of the world. Whoever follows me will never walk in darkness but will have the light of life" (John 8:12) and "I am the way, and the truth, and the life" (John 14:6). The Buddha directs me away from himself. The Christ invites me to himself. In the Four Reliances, the Buddha teaches, "Rely on the teaching not the teacher." In Christianity, the teaching is the Teacher.

The attitude of Jesus toward potential followers is clearly exemplified in a little scene in John's Gospel (John 1:35–42). John the Baptist commends Jesus to two of his own followers. They go to him and ask, "where are you staying?"

That is, "will you remain with us if we follow you?" Jesus responds, "Come and see." That is, he invites them to himself and invites them to "see," the great, controlling metaphor of John's Gospel, which means to perceive physically with the eyes, to understand with the mind and heart, and to be enlightened. The point for us is that Jesus invites people to himself for enlightenment.

I know from bitter experience my own inability to be my own lamp. Perhaps it is a lack of right effort on my part, and certainly my ignorance enters into the problem. But something else has always seemed to be at work, something that encouraged me toward "doing what I didn't want to do." In classical, Christian terms, "it" might be described as "original sin" inherent in my own flawed nature. Thus, the argument continues, I need the atonement effected by Jesus on the cross to redeem that "fallen nature." I am not sure that I entirely agree intellectually with this formulation, but I do know, practically, that I need help from outside myself. In the language of the spiritual child I am, "I need a God with skin on." To put the matter practically, I know what I should do (for example to sit or to practice detachment), but I need empowerment to achieve what I know. My hope for this is not in the human realm. This is a fundamental difference between Christianity and Buddhism. The Buddha teaches me to remain fully in the realm of human experience, but the Christ offers me a hope outside myself. "The hope of the Christian is . . . a hope *for* man, but it places its confidence in God, and not *in* man"[28] (italics mine).

Jesus Christ has not only "put skin on" and thereby redeemed and ennobled my flesh, but he invites me to profound identification with him, even participation in his very life. As Merton says, "God Himself lives in us, by His Holy Spirit."[29] Or as Brother David Steindl-Rast notes, "Christ lives in those who follow his path, and they live in him. . . . They are alive with his life."[30] Because he first invites me, not only can I come to him, but I can share and be empowered by his life to "do" what I "know." We Christians believe that Christ comes to us and dwells within us. We even make the outrageous and unlikely claim that we receive Christ's body into our physical and spiritual bodies in our eucharistic celebrations! In John's Gospel Jesus says, "those who eat my flesh and drink my blood abide in me, and I in them" (John 6:56). This is as shocking and audacious a claim today as it was when it was made in the first century of our era, and it means that "Christ is not simply an object of love and contemplation whom the Christian considers with devout attention: He is also 'the way, the truth and the life' so that for the Christian to be 'on the way' is to be 'in Christ.'"[31]

I believe that God "put skin on," among other reasons, to enable the human longing for and journey toward God. I, personally, have not been able to make that journey under my own steam. I need the empowerment of what the Apostle Paul calls "Christ in [us], the hope of glory" (Col. 1:27). I greatly appreciate and have learned much from the Buddha and his view of reality and his means of liberation, but the fullness of my being has responded to and been empowered by a personal invitation from Jesus to "come to me," "come and see." More precisely, I have had the experience that Brother David calls the "experience of being grasped or occupied"[32] by what the evangelical hymn of my youth calls the "Love that will not let me go." Note that Love "grasps" me. I respond to that glorious and terrible embrace, but I do not initiate it, and when I "grasp" at the one who offers it, I lose both the embrace and the Love that bestows it because real love cannot be based on human grasping or attachment. And this, I think, is very Buddhist.

Don't misunderstand me. I am not suggesting that my experience is, abstractly, either good or bad (although for me it has been very good, indeed) or even that it must needs be true for all. But this is my deepest reality. And in this "confession," I follow the example of the Buddha, who in effect says, "Be true to your own experience." So perhaps, in this very limited way, I am my own lamp. But the oil and the flame are Jesus Christ.

Shunryu Suzuki reminds us that true understanding comes out of emptiness: "When you study Buddhism, you should have a general house cleaning of your mind. You must take everything out of your room and clean it thoroughly. If it is necessary, you may bring everything back in again. You may want many things, so one by one you can bring them back. But if they are not necessary, there is no need to keep them."[33] More than once in my life the Buddha initiated an enormous spring cleaning. It was always good for me. I threw out a lot of useless stuff. I found some things I thought I'd lost and learned to treasure some things that had been there all along. I have immense gratitude to the Buddha and his Way. To change the metaphor, the Buddha offered me a raft. The raft, itself, was Jesus Christ. Or again, the Buddha pointed out a path that led me home. Jesus Christ was waiting for me on that road with arms outstretched and a feast waiting. Perhaps in this way the Buddha continues to bestow his enigmatic smile on me.

NOTES

1. And Fr. Hugo Enomiya-Lassalle, S.J. (1898–1990), one of the first Western Christians seriously to study and practice Buddhism, thought Christians could experience satori or enlightenment and integrate it into a Christian system of beliefs.

2. The matter of establishing the "historical Buddha" is nicely treated in Nagao Gadjin's "The Life of the Buddha" (*The Eastern Buddhist* 20 no. 2, 1987, pp. 2–7), from which I have taken the etymologies, and is critically examined in Whalen Lai's "The Search for the Historical Sakyamuni in Light of the Historical Jesus," *Buddhist-Christian Studies* 2 (1982), pp. 77–91.

3. Paul Tillich, *Christianity and the Encounter with World Religions* (New York: Columbia University Press, 1965), p. 97.

4. Jacques-Albert Cuttat, "Christian Experience and Oriental Spirituality," in *Concilium* 49 (New Tork: Paulist Press, 1969), p. 131. (Note: I prefer and use inclusive language in my own remarks but feel it a matter of accuracy to preserve the exact quotations of others.)

5. Michael Carrithers, *The Buddha* (New York: Oxford University Press, 1983); Nagao Gadjin, "The Life of the Buddha: An Interpretation," *Eastern Buddhist* 20 no. 2 (1987), pp. 1–31; David and Indrani Kalupahana, *The Way of Siddhartha* (Boulder: Shambala, 1982); F. W. Rawling, *The Buddha* (Cambridge: Cambridge University Press, 1975); H. W. Schumann, *The Historical Buddha* (London: Arkana, 1989).

6. Carrithers, *The Buddha,* pp. 11, 38.

7. Thomas Merton, "Buddhism and the Modern World," in *Mystics and Zen Masters* (New York: Delta, 1967), p. 286.

8. Carrithers, *The Buddha,* pp. 76–77.

9. Schumann, *The Historical Buddha,* p. 203.

10. His Holiness Tenzin Gyatso the Fourteenth Dalai Lama, *A Human Approach to World Peace* (London: Wisdom, 1988), p. 11.

11. Unless otherwise noted, all quotations of Christian scripture are from the New Revised Standard Version.

12. This, of course, assumes a fully actualized self to give. Many feminist writers have noted the problems of commending "self-giving" or "kenosis" or "service" as positive goals for women who may not have fully developed the self or who have been forced into service rather than being liberated and thus able to choose it. See, for example, Anne E. Carr, *Transforming Grace: Christian Tradition and Women's Experience* (San Francisco: HarperSanFrancisco, 1990).

13. Quoted in Schumann, *The Historical Buddha.* p. 62.

14. William Johnston, *Christian Zen: A Way of Meditation* (San Francisco: HarperSan Francisco, 1979), p. 15.

15. Walpola Rahula, *What the Buddha Taught* (New York: Grove Press, 1974), p. 70.

16. Tillich, *Christianity and the Encounter,* p. 81.

17. Shunryu Suzuki, *Zen Mind, Beginner's Mind* (New York: Weatherhill, 1976), pp. 29, 31.

18. Thomas Merton, "Mystics and Zen Masters," in *Mystics and Zen Masters* (New York: Delta Books, 1967), pp. 21–22.

19. Rahula, *What the Buddha Taught,* p. 17.

20. Schumann, *The Historical Buddha,* p. 138.

21. Merton, "Buddhism and the Modern World," pp. 286–87.

22. The phrase is Carrithers' and is found on p. 67 of *The Buddha.*

23. Quoted in Schumann, *The Historical Buddha,* p. 246.

24. See Thomas Merton, *Thoughts in Solitude* (New York: Farrar, Straus and Giroux, 1977), p. 83.

25. Quoted in Rahula, *What the Buddha Taught,* p. 130.

26. See, for example, Roy C. Amore, *Two Masters, One Message* (Nashville: Abingdon, 1978); Richard H. Drummond, *A Broader Vision: Perspectives on the Buddha and the Christ* (Virginia Beach, Virginia: A.R.E. Press, 1995); B. H. Streeter, *The Buddha and the Christ* (London: Macmillan, 1932); Steven C. Rockefeller and Donald Lopez Jr., eds., *The Christ and the Bodhisattva* (Albany: State University of New York Press, 1987).

27. Quoted in Rahula, *What the Buddha Taught,* p. 1.

28. Thomas Merton, preface to the Korean edition of *Life and Holiness* in *Introductions East and West,* Robert E. Daggy, ed. (Greensboro: Unicorn Press, 1981), p. 77.

29. Ibid.

30. Robert Aitken and David Steindl-Rast, *The Ground We Share: Everyday Practice Buddhist and Christian* (Liguori: Triumph Books, 1994), pp. 48–49.

31. Thomas Merton, preface to the Japanese edition of *Seeds of Contemplation* in *Introductions East and West,* p. 71.

32. Aitken and Steindl-Rast, *The Ground We Share,* p. 31.

33. Suzuki, *Zen Mind,* pp. 111–12.

BUDDHIST RESPONSES

If the Buddha Is So Great, Why Are These People Christians?

GRACE G. BURFORD

Prescott College

SINCE I BEGAN to study Buddhism as a Swarthmore College undergraduate and recognized my worldview as Buddhist, I have been puzzled about Christians who care about the Buddha. Why would a Christian care about the Buddha? I don't care a whit about Jesus, hence my difficulty in fathoming how a Christian could get all caught up in the Buddha. To put it another way, especially when I was first "turned on" to Buddhism (it was, after all, the seventies), I had trouble understanding why people who had studied Buddhism extensively, and whom I respected as otherwise quite smart and sensible, seemed to be doggedly determined to stay Christians! All of my Buddhism teachers in the course of my undergraduate and graduate study (with the notable exception of Walpola Rahula) fell in this category, it seemed—though we never really discussed it. Why didn't we discuss it? I did wonder about how they could dedicate their professional lives to—and be such effective teachers of—a tradition they did not believe in. If they were so taken by Buddhism, why did they hang on to Christianity? If they were Christians, why did they study and teach Buddhism? I guess I assumed it would be impertinent to pursue this question with my teachers and mentors; they were probably (justifiably) somewhat embarrassed by this backwards attachment to Christianity in the face of an obviously superior religion, Buddhism.

Why was I so ready to pitch Christianity and take up Buddhism, and my Buddhism teachers were not? Unlike these mentors, by the time I began my study of Buddhism I had already rejected the Christianity in which I was raised. I don't know why exactly I rejected Christianity so decisively; I had not experienced any trauma in Sunday school and had always loved the community my church provided. But during my junior year in high school I came to the point where I felt certain that I did not believe, nor had I ever really believed, a single word of the Christian creed I could recite so flawlessly. From that time until I discovered Buddhism, I made science-and-rationality my religion. In retrospect, I find it telling that the science I immersed myself in was astronomy—where there was plenty of room for mystery and wonder as I gazed two nights a week through Sproul Observatory's powerful twenty-four-inch refractor telescope into the night skies, in the coolest job a college student ever had. I will forever be an advocate of college course-distribution requirements, since it was these—and a friend who confided that "religion courses are not too bad"—that led me to take my first course from Donald Swearer. That same friend avers that I became a religion major because of my work at the telescope. Whatever the explanation, I felt fortunate to have run across Buddhism, to have found a mentor who could teach it so well, and to have discovered a religious path I could embrace enthusiastically. So why did my teacher hold back? Now *there* was a mystery.

I have confessed before in the pages of the *Buddhist-Christian Studies Journal* that my motives for participating in Buddhist-Christian dialogue and cross-religious discussions in general might seem ignoble, or at least not up to the usual expectations of this group. For some reason, my total abandonment of Christianity in my teen years has stuck (well into my forties, anyway). I honestly do not expect my predominantly Buddhist worldview to be enriched by learning more about Christianity. Nevertheless, I am fascinated with and continually enriched by other people and their religions. Despite my aversion to Christianity, I see that Christians are people, too. In fact, I am surrounded by Christians who, for better or worse, operate out of a Christian worldview. I am convinced we need each other, that we must work together to make the world a better place, especially in terms of the environmental crisis and social justice issues. So I am stuck with needing to understand Christians, especially the ones (such as the members of this group) who are willing to work with non-Christians like me.

These four essays help me to understand a certain group of Christians—those mysterious, intelligent people who study and experience Buddhism yet remain Christian—and these essays tell me, in part, what these Christians get out of Buddhism and why that is not enough for them.

First, it is clear from these essays that Elizabeth J. Harris, Terry Muck, and Bonnie Thurston are exactly the kind of people that baffle me. Harris says, "I remain a Christian, but the Buddha has become part of me." Muck identifies the Buddha as the subject of his scholarly study and Jesus as the object of his faith. Thurston credits the Buddha with leading her into ordination as a Christian minister and study and practice of Christian scripture. My own teacher, Donald K. Swearer, is less forthcoming in his essay as to his own faith, referring to it in the end as "dialogical" and "betwixt-and-between Christianity and Buddhism."

All of these articulate scholars have encountered the Buddha through both study and personal experience. They have spent years dedicated to reading Buddhist texts, encountering Buddhist art and iconography, and getting to know Buddhists. They love the wisdom and the compassion of the Buddha. They find confirmation of their own beliefs about the nature of reality and particularly about the challenges and promise of being human in the teachings and example of the Buddha. They are inspired professionally and personally by the Buddha they have come to know and appreciate.

"In complete honesty," Harris confesses, "I can say that I revere the Buddha," whom she describes as "the supreme embodiment of compassion and wisdom, the one who has seen into the nature of reality and the human predicament and has taught the path of liberation." Later in her essay Harris avows, "I too gain inspiration from the Buddha and hope that his compassion and wisdom will permeate my mind and heart." She can "draw into" herself the Buddha's message and "can benefit from the practice of mindfulness."

In a similar vein, Muck says, "I have loved the Buddha since I first began reading about him in graduate school at Northwestern University and listening to Walpola Rahula lecture about him in classes there." Because he sees the Buddha as "a teacher of religious genius . . . [and] a social reformer of great subtlety . . . [who is] pastoral," Muck maintains a significant and intellectually passionate "scholarly regard for the Buddha," whom he sees as "a great, good man." On a more personal note, Muck likes the Buddha for his dedication to finding spiritual truth, his "commonsense approach to communal living and institutional realities," and his "approach to personal spirituality." Muck's bronze Buddha image "fires [his] imagination for what is possible in the religious life." Muck concludes that he "couldn't think more highly of anyone."

Thurston frames her appreciation of the Buddha in terms of "six specific aspects of his life and teaching (his quest itself; his powers of analysis; his pragmatism; his moral vision; his compassion; and the outcome of living his 'way') that have attracted and taught" her. She also notes that two aspects of Buddhist practice have been "enormously helpful" to her, namely zazen meditation and detachment "from things, persons, even our sense of self." According to Thurston, this detachment counters desire, which "prevents my being at peace with what is." Thurston appreciates that "those who have heard of and responded to and lived out the Buddha's path have found a focus and equanimity that is impressive." She observes her own deep attraction to "the Buddhist goal of 'living radiantly in the present' and to the Buddha who both did it and demonstrated how to do it."

In Swearer's scholarly delineation of "the complexity of the figure of the Buddha within the varied and diverse traditions of Buddhism" in terms of universal and particular and wisdom and compassion, I detect a genuine personal appreciation of the Buddha as well. Swearer describes his participation in an all-night ritual reenactment of the Buddha's enlightenment as "one of the most moving experiences of my life." In it, he experienced how "the Buddha image consecration ritual transforms the Buddha image into a fusion of the universal dharma and the saint known as the Buddha."

So, my question seems justified: If they are all so moved and inspired by the Buddha, if their lives have been as enriched by their experiences of Buddhism as their essays indicate, why are all these well-informed people still Christians? Maybe it is a fluke, some kind of accident of what type of person agrees to write such essays, but there does seem to be a sort of consensus on this point among these Christians, one that I find very illuminating and surprisingly (to me, anyway) easy to understand.

Harris states, succinctly and clearly, "My encounter with the Buddha and what he taught has changed me irrevocably, but it has not destroyed my belief that there is 'other power' and such a thing as the grace of God." Thurston says, "I need the atonement effected by Jesus on the cross. . . . I need help from outside myself." For her, the Buddha's admonition "Be ye lamps unto yourselves" means we must "remain fully in the realm of human experience," whereas "the Christ offers me a hope outside myself." Muck finds that both his scholarly studies and his spiritual instincts detect significant differences between the Buddha and Jesus: the Buddha was human and taught us "the way to live life so that our problems can be overcome," whereas Jesus was divine and "taught us a way to live life that bears witness to the fact that Jesus, as God, has saved us from our sins." In other words, "The Buddha shows us the way, Jesus is the Way." Similarly, Thurston says, "the Buddha teaches, 'rely on the teaching not the teacher.' In Christianity, the teaching *is* the Teacher."

Of these four voices, only Swearer concludes with unifying rather than distinguishing comparisons of Buddhism and Christianity. For all of these authors, understanding and experience of Buddhism and the Buddha enriches their reflections on Christianity. But whereas Harris, Muck, and Thurston conclude with "why I am still a Christian," with an emphasis on the grace of God, Swearer notes that his study of how Buddhists view the Buddha has "enlarged my understanding of the paradox of the Incarnation, of God becoming Jesus the Christ, of the universal Logos becoming flesh, of the infinite becoming finite." In other words, he sees a parallel tension between the Buddha as both infinite and particular for Buddhists and the Christ as both infinite and particular for Christians. This parallel challenges the clear distinctions the other authors drew between the Buddha as teacher and Jesus as teaching. As Muck points out, there is an irony in the very way we refer to these two men, given the doctrines that present the Buddha as human (the teacher of the way) and Jesus as divine (the way): shouldn't we be calling them Gautama and the Christ?

For Harris, Muck, and Thurston, the Buddha teaches helpful ideas and practices, but in the end the saving grace of God that Jesus provides is not only crucial to their religious lives, it is also missing in Buddhism. For Swearer, despite his depth of intellectual understanding and personal experience of Buddhism, he returns to Christianity to "wrestle for personal meaning"—though he does not specify why, Buddhism alone is clearly not enough.

Muck suggests that socialization might explain his own different attitudes toward the Buddha and Jesus. He says, "I was raised to love Jesus, to believe in him." But this cannot be the whole story, or I would be a Christian. If the difference comes down to a Buddhist model of human power to follow a religious path toward wisdom and compassion versus a Christian model of divine intervention through the power of grace for universal salvation, I can understand both why Christians remain Christians even when they encounter Buddhism and why I am not the least tempted to return to Christianity. These are two very different approaches to religious life. Given the very real element of personal devotion to the Buddha in Buddhism and the distancing of Jesus through Christian worship and dogma, clearly not everyone would distinguish Buddhism and Christianity this way. But I do, and Harris, Muck, and Thurston do, and it was Swearer who observed in an interview for the film *Be Ye Lamps Unto Yourselves* that although there are many similarities between Buddhism and Christianity, the central images of the Buddha sitting under a tree meditating and the Christ suffering on the cross to save humanity reflect very different approaches to the religious life. If I imaginatively reverse my response to this dichotomy of religious options, I come much closer to solving the conundrum that has puzzled me for over twenty years. For these Christians, as for myself, ultimately either one or the other model works, but not both.

Once when I had been studying Buddhism for a few years, I was enthusiastically describing to my mother this Buddhist religion that I thought was so wonderful. She remarked, with equal enthusiasm, "What that religion needs is a good savior!" I laughed, easily, completely unthreatened by her critique, precisely because I felt such a deep certainty that this was the very area in which—for me—Buddhism provided such a great leap forward in my religious life and represented a major improvement over Christianity. I do not know why the Buddhist model appeals to me so deeply. I can certainly relate to Thurston's feelings of inadequacy in the face of the central religious task.

But for me it is inherently a task I must do and not have done for me. I appreciate help, and I know that nothing I do is truly independent (see the Buddhist explanation of dependent co-arising). I might want some cosmic grace, even. But I don't conceive of that grace as coming from a personal God who saved all of humanity by incarnating in Jesus, or as being required by some innate deficiency in myself that has to be fixed by someone else. For me, grace lies in the interdependence of things, and that is enough. So give me a map, lend me your car (or raft?), show me a shortcut, even protect me along the way if you can—but do not make the trip for me!

Contrasting Images
of the Buddha

Taitetsu Unno
Smith College

ALL THE CHRISTIAN writers express a deep and sympathetic appreciation for the historical Sakyamuni Buddha, demonstrating some of the positive fruits of interreligious dialogue. But—speaking as a practicing Buddhist— their views appear to be focused on the human face of the Buddha and scant attention is paid to what might be called the numinous. It is this dimension of his enlightenment experience that constitutes his very being and the reason for his appeal far beyond the borders of India. This sense of the sacred, the transhistorical, inspired the great civilizations of Asia and today attracts world- wide attention to the Buddhist path of liberation and freedom.

Terry Muck makes an ironic allusion to the respective lives of the Buddha and of the Christ. He states that "Official Christian dogma teaches that Jesus was divine, a part of the Trinity, three gods in one: Father, Son, and Holy Spirit. Buddhist teachings dogmatize a different understanding of the Buddha—that he was human through and through," but a reversal occurs in later history: "The popular Buddhist approach to the Buddha tends to produce a 'godlike' Buddha in a religious tradition that insists on his humanity, and the popular Christian approach to Jesus tends to produce a very human Jesus in a religious tradition that insists on Jesus' divinity. It is almost as if the populace has decided to emphasize what the buddholo- gians and theologians have decreed secondary. The evidence for this reversal is everywhere."

This may be a valid observation, but the truth of the matter might not be so simple. That is, both religious figures may combine the practical and the spiritual in different, complex ways and, depending on the historical lens, a person may see one aspect and not the other. At any rate, in this paper I wish to note that Sakyamuni Buddha is more than simply "human, through and through."

Rudolph Otto was the first to use "numinous" as a religious category to describe Christian and Hindu experience, but it also can be applied to the Buddhist case. This is so if we subscribe to one of its basic characteristics: the quality of the *inexpressible*—"in the sense that it completely eludes apprehension in terms of concepts."[1] In Buddhist literature we have an abundance of words suggesting this fact: the unconditioned, formless, ineffable, inconceivable, unthinkable, unattainable, indefinable, immeasurable, and so on.

In order to understand the numinous fully, Otto writes that a person "must be guided and led on by consideration and discussion of the matter through the ways of his own mind, until he reaches the point at which 'the numinous' in him perforce begins to stir, to start into life and into consciousness."[2] He continues: "The arising of the numinous from beyond discursive consciousness is central to the Buddha's enlightenment experience. This point has been overlooked and has caused misunderstanding, as noted by John Ross Carter: 'One is told repeatedly that one has to work out one's own salvation—this is treated as a corollary to there being no savior or savior god. This has been pounded into the English-reading audience to such an extent that one has failed to discern what Theravada Buddhism has long known—one does not work out one's own salvation or liberation or release.'"[3]

In the Theravada classic, *Visudhimagga*, the ultimate awakening does not result from human calculation. According to Mahinda Palihawadana, it comes from the "arising of *magga*." *Magga* is the "path" in the eightfold scheme (*ariya attahangika magga*), but it has a further connotation: "the moment of spiritual change as well as the event and the content of the mind at the moment."[4] He sums up this process by enumerating the fourfold goal of Theravada life. The first three are well known—*sila, samadhi,* and *lokiya panna*. There is also the fourth, which is crucial but often overlooked: supramundane or *lokuttara panna*. The first three are preliminaries to the fourth realization: "Personal effort is only the 'setting' for the realization of the highest religious truth, that the highest realization can take place only when effort ceases to be, having exhausted its scope and having brought about the knowledge that it too is a barrier to be broken down."[5]

Carter also underscores this point when he writes: "One nudges the limit of possible human action, one witnesses the falling away of calculation, the cultivation of wholesome actions (*kusalakamma*) that might count as it were toward the arising of the path, *magga*."[6]

What, then, is this arising of *magga?* The arising "1) discards vitiating psychic characteristics, 2) provides first-hand acquaintance with transcendent reality, and 3) gives a profound understanding of truth. It is therefore spontaneous generation of a qualitative newness of being, a true psychical *mutation* which raises one from one's weaknesses and brings on a total change."[7]

Such an experience leads to an awareness similar to that indicated by Bonnie Thurston: "We Christians believe that Christ comes to us and dwells in us." While not the same thing, a senior monk in Sri Lanka, as quoted by Elizabeth Harris, states: "I like to have my Buddha living within me. His enlightenment was personal to him, but as the Mahayanists or Zen Buddhists would say there's enlightenment in every grain of sand. Why not within me? So I've already got a pacesetter, the Buddha, in my heart so that it keeps inspiring me all of the time."

One of the difficulties of properly understanding Buddhism is its reliance on the experiential rather than on the discursive or conceptual, which tends to objectify, reify, and absolutize words and concepts. This characteristic of Asian religious traditions led Cardinal Paul Shan Kuohsi of Taiwan to alert conveners at the Synod of Asia: "Missionaries to Asia must keep in mind the cultural context that places much more emphasis on an experience of the divine than on the intellectual."[8]

To borrow the language of William James, we can say that the Buddha "turns away from abstraction and inefficiency; from verbal solutions, from bad a priori reason, from fixed principles, closed systems and pretended absolutes and origins. . . . It means the open air and possibilities of nature, as against dogma, artificiality, and pretense of finality in truth."[9] But this does not exclude the numinous, the transhistorical, or the transcendent: "not a deity *in concreto,* not a superhuman person, but the immanent divinity in things, the essentially spiritual structure of the universe."[10]

In Mahayana Buddhism, the numinous quality is pervasive among the multitudes of Buddhas and bodhisattvas. This is especially true in the case of Amida Buddha of the Pure Land tradition. Donald Swearer discusses the pleading of Brahma Samapatti, who requests the Buddha to teach suffering humanity, and concludes, "This story can be seen as the anticipation of the cosmic dimension of the compassion of Amida Buddha in the Japanese Pure Land tradition." John Ross Carter also speaks of the parallel between the "arising of *magga*" and the Shin Buddhist teaching of *shinjin*, faith as true entrusting, taught by Honen (1133–1212) and Shinran (1173–1263).[11] While the Theravada and Pure Land traditions are historically and doctrinally worlds apart, experientially they share the working of "other power," a synonym for Amida Buddha.

In order to make the connection from Sakyamuni to Amida Buddha, we must turn to the definition of *dhamma* or *dharma* and its evolution in East Asia. Although such a huge task remains to be undertaken, we can trace the basic trajectory in the words of Buddhadasa Bhikkhu: "The Buddha in everyday language refers to the historical, enlightened being, Gotama Buddha. It refers to a physical man of flesh and bone who was born in India over two thousand years ago, died, and was cremated. This is the meaning of the Buddha in everyday language. Considered in terms of Dhamma language, however, the word 'Buddha' refers to the Truth that the historical Buddha realized and taught, the Dhamma itself. The Buddha said, 'He who sees the Dhamma sees the Enlightened One. He who sees the Enlightened One sees the Dhamma. One who sees not the Dhamma, though he grasps at the robe of the Enlightened One, cannot be said to have *seen* the Enlightened One.'"[12]

When this focus on *dhamma* is extended and developed, it evolves into the *trikaya* of Mahayana Buddhism. The Pure Land Buddhists see the historical Buddha through *trikaya*, the threefold manifestation of Buddhahood, as follows. First is *dharmakaya*, body of true reality that is beyond discursive consciousness. Responding to the cries of suffering beings, it manifests itself as *sambhogakaya* or Amida Buddha. This truth is proclaimed in history by *nirmanakaya*, incarnated body of the historical Buddha, the primary source of all the teachings of Buddhism.

This embodiment of *dhamma/dharma*, whether in Theravada or Mahayana, is central to the radical self-sufficiency found in the injunction,

"Be ye lamps unto yourselves." The self here is not the unenlightened ego self, but the enlightened non-ego self imbued with *dhamma,* as clearly underscored in the subsequent passage, "Hold fast to the *dhamma* as a lamp. Seek salvation alone in the *dhamma.*"[13] While Pali literature speaks of "self as lamp" (*atta-dipa*), the Sanskrit uses "self as island" (*atma-dvipa*).

This distinction between the unenlightened and enlightened self is critical to the proper understanding the of Four Reliances, the first of which states: "Rely on the teaching and not on the teacher." The admonition here is not to rely on just another human being caught up in samsara, but on the *dhamma.* If it is completely realized in a teacher, as in the case of Sakyamuni Buddha, the teacher and *dhamma* are inseparable. Hence the proclamation, "He who sees the *dhamma* sees the Enlightened One. He who sees the Enlightened One sees the *dhamma.*"

NOTES

1. Rudolph Otto, *The Idea of the Holy: An Inquiry into the Non-rational Factor in the Idea of the Divine and its Relation to the Rational* (London: Oxford University Press, 1971), p. 5.

2. Ibid, p. 7.

3. John Ross Carter, "The Arising of Magga and Shiunjin," *The Pure Land, New Series* no. 4 (December 1987), p. 97.

4. Mahinda Palihawadana, "Is There a Theravada Buddhist Idea of Grace?" in *Christian Faith in a Religiously Plural World,* Donald Dawe and John Carman, eds. (Maryknoll, New York: Orbis Books, 1978), p. 194n.

5. Carter, "Arising of Magga" p. 99.

6. Ibid.

7. Palihawadana, "Is There a Theravada Buddhist Idea of Grace?" p. 192.

8. "Asian Bishops' Synod Discusses Interreligious Dialogue," *Bulletin of Monastic Interreligious Dialogue,* 59 (Spring 1998), p. 12.

9. William James, *Essays in Pragmatism* (New York: Harper, 1955), p. 21.

10. William James, *The Varieties of Religious Experience* (New York: Vintage Books, 1990), p. 36.

11. See article cited in endnote 4.

12. Buddhadasa Bhikkhu, *Toward the Truth,* Donald K. Swearer, ed. (Philadelphia: Westminster Press, 1971), pp. 58–59. Also partially quoted in Swearer, pp. 4–5.

13. See *The Teaching of the Compassionate Buddha,* Edwin Burtt, ed. (New York: North American Library, 1955), p. 49. This translation renders *dhamma* as "truth."

Buddhist Books on Jesus

TERRY C. MUCK,

Austin Presbyterian Theological Seminary

The Dalai Lama. *The Good Heart: A Buddhist Perspective on the Teachings of Jesus.* Boston: Wisdom Publications, 1996. $24.00. 210 pages.

Thich Nhat Hanh. *Living Buddha, Living Christ.* New York: Riverhead Books, 1995. $20.00. 210 pages.

Kenneth S. Leong. *The Zen Teachings of Jesus.* New York: Crossroad Publishing, 1995. $14.95. 204 pages.

"Who do you say I am?" Jesus asked his Jewish disciple. Peter responded with a Jewish answer: "You are the Messiah" (Matt. 16:15–16). Christians over the centuries have continued to ask Jesus' question. As Jaroslav Pelikan shows us in *Jesus Through the Centuries,* we have continued to add richness and breadth and depth to the disciples's first answer: the Messiah Jesus is the Son of God, the Good Shepherd, the Lord of the Harvest, the Liberator.

Some modern Jewish scholars, who reject their brother Peter's assessment of Jesus as Messiah, have nevertheless seen Jesus as an important religious and historical figure: Jesus as everyday Jew, Jesus as rabbinical teacher. Muslim scholars see in Jesus a great prophet of Allah and accord him religious respect as a fundamental tenet of their religious tradition.

Given this history and the plurality of religions in the United States today, it is perhaps inevitable that other religions, even those not historically connected to Christianity, would recognize the pivotal nature of Jesus of Nazareth for Christian faith and human history and comment on his life and times.

Recently three prominent Buddhists have written books assessing Jesus from a Buddhist point of view. These three books help us begin to articulate a complex and not always consistent answer to the question, "Who do Buddhists think Jesus was?"

THE GOOD-HEARTED JESUS

ARGUABLY, THE MOST famous Buddhist in the world is the Dalai Lama, the spiritual leader of Tibetan Buddhists. In some ways it is both misleading and un-Buddhist that one man represent the world Buddhist community. Buddhism is much less hierarchically structured than Christianity and one of its principle teachings, *anatta* or no-self, discourages individualism. Further, Tibetan Buddhism represents only one aspect of the world Buddhist community and a smallish one at that.

In other ways the Dalai Lama's notoriety is understandable. He represents an oppressed people—the Dalai Lama himself is in exile in India, driven out by the Chinese colonization of Tibet. The plight of Tibet has become a *cause celebre* among the Western intelligentsia and several Hollywood personalities. Further, the Dalai Lama is charismatic, dedicated, and wise. His celebrity is earned. So his book, *The Good Heart: A Buddhist Perspective on the Teachings of Jesus,* merits consideration by Christian readers.

The book itself is a collection of eight Bible studies on Jesus' words given by the Dalai Lama at a Buddhist-Christian interfaith conference. He reads the text, giving a Buddhist gloss on the content, and in the process, on Jesus himself. Each commentary is followed by a Christian respondent's thoughts on both the passage and the Dalai Lama's exegesis. Thus this is an exegetical approach to understanding the historical Jesus. Using Jesus' words, filtered through a Buddhist worldview, the Dalai Lama paints a biographical portrait.

The focus of the picture is on Jesus' teachings about mental attitude and Jesus' own mental attitude. For the Dalai Lama, Jesus models a "spiritually mature, good, and warm hearted person" (80). We should emulate Jesus in this lifestyle.

The way to do this is through meditation. The Dalai Lama sees the common ground between the two religions to be meditation not philosophy. He freely acknowledges the philosophical differences. He does not attempt to reduce the two religious systems to a lowest common denominator abstraction (73). But because both deal with the life and teachings of two men, Jesus and Buddha, who each worked hard to teach disciples how to develop "good hearts," we can agree on the importance of the devotional life and realize the benefits of that particular focus—mutual good will.

Mutual good will means the two religions can practice mutual appreciation toward one another, recognize our potentially complementary nature even as we each fulfill our "missionary" callings through advocacy. The goal is a freedom on both sides to champion the gospel of Jesus and the dhamma of Gautama without disparaging the other's path. The religious "practitioner should set out and attempt to communicate (their practice) to others so that they to can share the experience" (95).

How can this be done in a world where cutthroat competition is the rule? The Dalai Lama begins by personifying this cooperative competition. He is very humble about his attempts to understand Jesus and his words—"this is *my* understanding of Christian theology," he says with a twinkle at one point (56). He is not apologetic about what he offers in the way of commentary; still, he never loses sight of the fact that this is another religious tradition's scriptures. In the end he defers to Christians' self understandings where they might conflict with his own.

He obviously believes others can learn this good heartedness. He recommends Buddhist and Christian scholars meet and talk regularly. He is enthusiastic about the rich conversations already taking place among Buddhist monastic meditators and Christian monastics. He promotes pilgrimages to one another's holy sites. All of these things, he believes, will deepen friendships among adherents of the two traditions.

The Jesus that emerges from this exegesis is a person remarkably similar to the Dalai Lama himself: someone able to hold passionate commitments about the religious life, to advocate those teachings to others, but to do so in such a way that unifies people around our common humanness rather than destructively dividing us over our important differences. The key to combining this passionate commitment and unswerving openness is the good heart.

THE ENGAGED JESUS

THICH NHAT HANH presents a different vision of Jesus in *Living Buddha, Living Christ*. Like the Dalai Lama, he too likes Jesus. He likes him very much and does not hesitate to tell readers, especially Christian readers, why. Yet this is a very different approach to Jesus than the one taken by the Dalai Lama.

If the Dalai Lama's approach could be likened to that of a biblical exegete (or more precisely, a Bible study leader), Thich Nhat Hanh's resembles a philosopher of religion. He attempts to distill from what Christians say and believe about Jesus Christ a picture that comports well with a similar picture of Gautama Buddha—someone interested in the health and welfare of all sentient beings. This picture does not emerge from Jesus' meditative practice but from what Jesus taught and did in his public life.

There is a certain congruence between this picture of Jesus and the foci of Thich Nhat Hanh's life. He practices Zen Buddhism, but a Zen heavily influenced by a life of social activism. As chairman of the Vietnamese Buddhist Peace Delegation during the Vietnam War, he was nominated by Martin Luther King for the Nobel Peace Prize. Today, like the Dalai Lama, he lives in exile from his home country, Vietnam. From his base in France he carries on his teachings of peaceful coexistence by writing, lecturing, and leading retreats.

Thich Nhat Hanh is interested in emphasizing the activist side of Jesus' ministry and that interest emerges in the descriptions he gives of how Buddhism, true Buddhism, and Christianity, true Christianity, relate to one another. He uses his philosophy of religion approach to demonstrate how congruent Buddhism and Christianity are to one another on this point, and how congruent the life and teachings of Jesus and the life and teachings of Gautama are when it comes to their core messages: "I do not think there is that much difference between Christians and Buddhists" (154). This philosophical/theological focus gives a certain tone to this book.

First, Thich Nhat Hanh is more interested in right understanding than the good heart. By all accounts, mind you, Thich Nhat Hanh has a good heart and endorses others' good hearts. But when it comes to establishing a base for cooperative action among Buddhist and Christians (and this is his goal), Jesus' casting the money changers out of the temple is the paradigmatic act, not the meditative reflectiveness of the Beatitudes.

Second, this understanding is not understanding for understanding's sake. It is understanding discovered in practice. This reflects both a core Zen focus on the importance of practice as the base of the religious life, but also extends the idea of practice, praxis, in a way not unsimilar to Christian liberation theologians' understanding of praxis. Traditionally when Zen masters say practice they mean mindful sitting, zazen. Practice, yes, but not social activism. Thich Nhat Hanh extends the meaning without giving up on meditation.

Third, the content of this joint practice is what we together must do in order to address the injustices of human political and economic structures. That is not only Thich Nhat Hanh's common ground, but, he argues, the essence of both religious traditions. "When Jesus said, 'I am the way,' he meant that to have a true relationship with God, you must practice his way. In the Acts of the Apostles, the early Christians always spoke of their faith as 'the Way.' To me, 'I am the way" is a better statement than 'I know the way'" (55).

This approach to Jesus and Christianity adds distinction to this book. In arguing the case, Thich Nhat Hanh doesn't hesitate to tell Christians what the true core of Jesus' teachings is. He explains Christianity to Christians. "Jesus taught a gospel of nonviolence. Is the church today practicing the same by its presence and behavior?" (72). He does not hesitate to exclude those who do not agree with his right understanding of Jesus' message. One suspects he would do the same to fellow Buddhists in reference to Gautama's teachings.

The effects of this approach when it comes to interreligious relations are profound. Whereas the Dalai Lama uses the concept of the good heart as a vehicle to promote interreligious harmony while continuing to recognize the differences between the two religious traditions, Thich Nhat Hanh presses his argument about a common core to unite Christians and Buddhists who agree with his analysis, while recognizing that some Buddhists and Christians don't see this analysis as central to the two traditions. In other words, the key division is not between Buddhists and Christians per se, but between Buddhist/Christians who see human flourishing as the essence of the two traditions and Buddhist/ Christians who don't. This approach is well illustrated by Christian Trappist monk Thomas Merton's laudatory comment about Thich Nhat Hanh: "Thich Nhat Hanh is more my brother than many who are nearer to me in race and nationality, because he and I see things in exactly the same way" (cover copy).

ZEN MASTER JESUS

IN THE *Zen Teachings of Jesus,* Kenneth S. Leong is neither exegete nor philosopher of religion. He is, first, a comparative religionist and, second, an apologist for Zen Buddhism, or more precisely, for a Zen way of apprehending the world. As comparative religionist he chooses a category from one religious tradition (in this case Zen Buddhism) and sets about showing resonances of that category in the teachings and practices of another religious tradition, in this case Christianity. He does not work toward a common ground amidst diversity (as did the Dalai Lama), nor does he seek out a dynamic equivalency between two traditions (as did Thich Nhat Hanh) but he argues for a recognition that "Zen is everywhere" (43). In Leong's approach, it would be appropriate to call Jesus "an anonymous Zen Buddhist."

Just as the Jesus depicted by both the Dalai Lama and Thich Nhat Hanh bore a remarkable resemblance to the interests of the two authors, so Leong's Jesus shows a great affinity with him. Leong was converted from Christianity to Zen Buddhism at the age of sixteen: "I left Jesus to search for the Tao when I was sixteen. Now I am forty and realize I could have found the Tao in Jesus" (11). He now teaches Zen practice at Wainwright House in Rye, New York, encouraging Christians to reinterpret their religious tradition in light of Zen.

Most of the book details the nature of what can be found in Jesus that is so appropriate to Zen meditation. He is especially interested in discovering what he calls "the lost dimensions" of Jesus' spirituality, particularly his joy, humor, and poetry. He especially misses our lack of appreciation of Jesus' sense of humor. We are far too serious about Jesus, he asserts, and this inhibits our ability to practice everyday spirituality, because seriousness is a sign of an overactive ego (14).

In order to unearth Jesus' Zen side, two things must be done. First, certain ways of apprehending the Christian gospels must be seen for what they are: blocks to fully understanding the radical nature of Jesus' teachings and, in some cases, actual perversions of the teaching itself. In this category, Leong is especially critical of Western approaches to rationality and truth, which he calls absurd and tyrannical (13). This leads to a literal way of reading the Bible, which turns out to be, in Leong's eyes, a form of illiteracy. We miss Jesus' message in the process. Leong is also opposed to all forms of institutional religion, because institutional life filters out "soul competency," the ability to feel and intuit Jesus rather than rotely understanding him.

The second task, the more positive side, is to give a Zen-style reading of Jesus' life and teachings. He begins by spending two chapters attempting to describe what Zen is: not a religion as much as a mental culture, a way of approaching life. Chapters 3 through 11 bring interesting Zen insights to bear on familiar gospel stories in ways that are not critical of the stories so much as they are encouragements to read them from a new point of view. A new picture of Jesus emerges from this reading and reminds us how much our understanding of Jesus is colored by the cultural worldview we bring to the reading.

OBSERVATIONS

THREE DIFFERENT READINGS. In some ways, one can see the similarities, owing to the fact that all three authors are Buddhists and are unapologetic about letting their religious categories shape their readings. In other, and equally important ways perhaps, one can see sharp differences in the way Jesus is portrayed. Still, we can make some common observations:

1. *All three portraits are properly appreciative of what a great man Jesus was.* All three recognized Jesus as a great teacher; Hanh "came to know Jesus as a great teacher" (99) from his early friendship with Christians and his early contact with French missionaries in Vietnam, although this contact made appreciating some other elements of Christianity difficult (5). Leong's whole premise is that Jesus was a great, albeit unrecognized, teacher of Zen.

In addition, all three recognize in one way or another that Jesus was a pivotal figure in human history. Hanh perhaps pays him the highest compliment by pairing him with the Buddha as the two most pivotal figures in all human history (45). Leong considers Jesus the most famous person in human history (11).

They also recognize and appreciate Jesus' role as a spiritual figure, not just in the public sense, but in his essence. The Dalai Lama claims his reverence for Jesus stems from his understanding of Jesus as a fully enlightened human being, a bodhisattva. Although it is difficult to know just what he means by using this language, Leong says, "we can certainly see Jesus as Savior, Messiah, Son of God" (14).

It may be only common sense that anyone who writes an entire book on a person will have a high regard for that person. Still, it is important to rehearse the answers, the positive affirmations given to Jesus. The answer to this question might help uncover any inappropriate religious or cultural biases being brought to the readings. All three authors pass the test on this score. Although Hanh and Leong, especially, are critical of certain understandings of Jesus and certain types of followers of Jesus, neither is critical of Jesus himself.

2. *They don't see Jesus the way confessing Christians see Jesus.* Or put another er way, when I read these descriptions as a confessing Christian, there is something missing. I am not sure it is "my" Jesus they are talking about. As we have seen, these authors are properly appreciative, but they are not confessionally committed to what Jesus stands for. So what's missing in these portraits?

Jean Luc Marion in *God Without Being* makes an interesting distinction between idols and icons, a distinction that might help us in answering this question. An idol acts like a mirror, reflecting as much of our own understandings of a subject as of the essence of the subject itself. An icon propels us toward the essence by encouraging us to look through and beyond the graphic representation, on toward the thing in itself.

Perhaps it is that distinction we find here. We have already noted above the irony that Jesus turns out to be, in each author's description, a person interested in the very things the authors are most interested in: Jesus the meditator *par excellence* for the Dalai Lama, Jesus the social activist for Thich Nhat Hanh; Jesus the Zen teacher for Kenneth Leong. These are idols, if we can use Marion's images, idols in the best sense. They are not necessarily inaccurate, and they are not meant to belittle Jesus by any means. But they mirror what these Buddhist authors see as important qualities, qualities they think we should endorse and emulate. As the Dalai Lama movingly notes, we can know Jesus in his depths when we achieve a peaceful equanimity, a condition of non-attachment that Buddhist meditation so effectively creates (67). Or as Hanh says, we are all of the same reality as Jesus (44).

Christian descriptions of Jesus often have this mirror quality also, of course. But the best Christian theological and devotional writing also has the icon quality, the ability to point us toward the transcendent reality of Jesus, the surplus of meaning, the mystery that we can only experience in our day to day walk with the risen Christ. As the Dalai Lama puts it, "the meaning of the themes [he highlights in Jesus' words], may be slightly different [from Christian meanings] because of the uniqueness that is accorded to Jesus as the Son of God" (89).

3. *All three authors appropriate Jesus for their own ends.* And of course those ends happen to be Buddhist ends, although all three probably would want to make the case that those "Buddhist" ends also happen to coincide with more general human ends. Again we should not be surprised at this, nor should we assume it is sinister in any way. As Christians, when we read the life story of the Buddha and contemplate his teachings, we naturally do so from a Christian point of view.

Still, the fact that such a reading is inevitable does not mean that we should accept such readings uncritically. The question is not really whether or not such authors appropriate Jesus for their own ends. Even Christian authors do that. The real question is how they do it. Basically there are three roads such an appropriation can take.

First, one can appropriate by *reduction*: limit Jesus to one aspect and claim that that is the key to understanding his person and work. Jesus is a great teacher of Zen principles, and that is the key to understanding him. Or one can reduce by leveling, by claiming that Jesus is just one of a general class of religious teachers/leaders. Or that although Jesus may not offer the *same* path to God, he does offer *one* path to God.

All three authors, to some extent, practice this kind of reduction when it comes to Jesus. Leong sees in Jesus a Zen teacher and little more. He is a teacher of Zen but not a teacher who inspired two thousand years of Christian orthodoxy (17–18). The Dalai Lama wants to endorse Jesus' meditative practices without necessarily endorsing the logic and rationale behind those practices (45). By saying that we should not spend our life "tasting just one kind of fruit," Hanh seems to imply there are many religious fruits of equal value, and we should not be afraid to sample as many as we want, measuring them by how much they contribute to peace and justice (2).

Second, one can appropriate by *changing* the life and teachings of a religious founder in order to make them compatible with one's own world view. None of these three authors seems to fall into this camp. All work very hard to understand Jesus as he truly was and as the Christian tradition has understood him. All three are well informed regarding the biblical record of Jesus' words and base their arguments on those words. We may disagree with some of their interpretations, but most of us disagree with a lot of Christian commentary on Jesus' life and times.

A great irony emerged as I read these three books. These Buddhist authors showed far more respect for the traditional historical Jesus and the devotional attachment Christians have for him than do the Christian exegetes who make up the Jesus Seminar. These Buddhists see Jesus as one of the world's great religious resources; the Jesus Seminar Christians see Jesus as a problem to solve, a cipher to get right. What the Dalai Lama, Thich Nhat Hanh, and Kenneth Leong lack in confessional commitment they balance by their good hearted desire to see Jesus as Christians see Jesus.

Third, one can appropriate by *using* the lessons one learns from another religion or religious figure to augment the teachings of one's own religion. Again, all three authors seem to do this. They see the richness of Jesus' teaching as a mother lode of wisdom for their respective Buddhist constituencies. As we have noted, they all three carry significant take aways for their Buddhist lives because of their study of Jesus.

Their motives go deeper than that, however. They also think Christians can learn significant lessons, without ceasing to be Christians, from these Buddhist readings of Jesus. This is a truth that we need to be reminded of constantly. Christian theology has always developed out of missional settings, out of contact with other religions and worldviews. It is not a matter of simply comparing or leveling all religions. It is a matter of Christians reappropriating, in appropriate ways, lessons learned from these Buddhist appropriations of our most sacred heart. How does the Dalai Lama's Buddhist understanding of Jesus' good heart enrich my Christian understanding of Jesus? How does Thich Nhat Hanh's Buddhist understanding of Jesus as human liberator deepen my Christian understanding of Jesus? How does Kenneth Leong's Buddhist understanding as Jesus as Zen master broaden my Christian understanding of Jesus?

Perhaps that is the way we should, in the end, view these fine books. We should not dismiss them out of hand as suspect, non-Christian poachings on themes more properly reserved for Christians alone. We should rejoice in the interest Jesus of Nazareth creates whenever people are made aware of his story. It is a powerful story.

As a graduate student at Northwestern University I studied with a great Buddhist scholar from Sri Lanka, Walpola Rahula. After two years of study with him, I asked him one day at lunch, "Have you read the Bible?"

"I have read the gospels," he replied.

"What did you think?" I asked.

"When I read the story of Jesus, I cried. He was a great, great man."

The story of Jesus, when read fairly by Christian and non-Christian alike, is a powerful story. The essence of Christianity is to share that story. We should rejoice to have these three excellent records of how it has affected three Buddhist readers. We can learn from them.